AF469687

SPORTS-ARBITRAGE

How To Place Riskless Bets and Create Tax Free Investments

Rajeev Shah

www.sportsarbitrageworld.com

Published by Lulu.com

ISBN: 978-1-4092-0478-7

78 York Street, London, W1H 1DP
www.amarcode.com

To Mum and Dad, who taught me to care and reason,
and to Pushpam who makes it all matter

About the author

Rajeev Shah spent most of the 1990's as a foreign exchange dealer and futures trader in the City of London. Leaving the City in 1997 to focus on new opportunities unfolding as the Internet became mainstream, he discovered a rapidly growing range of arbitrage opportunities created in the online sports-betting markets. After a year of research, during which he ran a highly successful private sports-arbitrage trading fund, in 1998 he created the world's first and foremost sports-arbitrage trading software. Today, Rajeev focuses his attention on helping new traders through his articles, books, seminars and software innovations on his website www.sportsarbitrageworld.com

About the contributors

Alan Seymour is 57 years old and, until late 2001, worked as a civil engineer in Essex. He took an early retirement & has been a sports-arbitrage trader since

Adam Barnfield is 29 years old and works as an IT consultant in Manchester. He specialises in soccer arbitrage

Amir Bansil is 48 years old and runs an one-man accountancy practice from home. He has been trading sports-arbitrage successfully since 2006

Mark Dawson is 45 and began trading sports-arbitrage after leaving the City in 2003. He specialises in finding arbitrage trades "off the beaten track"

Andy Summervale has been trading part-time since 2005 & specialises in soccer arbitrage. He is the originator of a remarkable technique that can be used to include accumulator bets within arbitrage trades

Fiona Hayes is a golf-specialist who has been trading part-time since the first half of 2007

Patrick Goodman started trading part-time in 2000. He moved to full-time trading in 2001 and recently emigrated to Australia, where he splits his time between sports-arbitrage trading and kite-surfing. He specialises in betting-exchange arbitrage strategies

Simon Ferguson is a full-time trader specialising in middles and other more obscure forms of sports-arbitrage trading

Preface

This book is a distillation of the experiences I have gained over 10 years as a sports-arbitrage trader, information revealed during question and answer sessions held with visitors to my sports-arbitrage website www.sportsarbitrageworld.com and various interviews & discussions I have had with a number of the most successful sports-arbitrage professionals in the UK.

The gaming industry is one of the largest, and fastest growing, industries in the world. Its growth has mushroomed in the past decade thanks to the Internet. For the most part, it remains true that in the long-run, the house always wins. However, for some time now, a few individuals have been taking advantage of little-known anomalies in the global sports-betting markets in order to make guaranteed, risk-free profits at the expense of the bookmakers.

These individuals are sports-arbitrage traders.

This book sets out towards 2 goals: to teach the novice reader all there is to know before embarking on his or her sports-arbitrage trading project, and to teach experienced traders some of the more complex techniques used by professionals.

Whether you are a novice or experienced trader, my hope is that this book will bring you increased profits from your sports-arbitrage trading project.

Rajeev Shah
London 2009

Table of Contents

Introduction

Arbitrage is a trading technique whereby exactly offsetting positions are taken in a market simultaneously but at different prices. The difference in price represents an immediate risk-free profit that is independent of the subsequent movement in price of the instruments traded. This technique has long been used in financial markets, which can be difficult for non-professionals to access.

However, thanks to the internet, with the proliferation of online bookmakers across the world competing for the multi-billion dollars spent on gambling each year, numerous arbitrage situations, also referred to as surebets, scalps and risk free bets, are created everyday in sports-betting.

The opportunities are almost endless and always renewing themselves, event after event. When bookmakers compile their odds, they are merely reflecting their opinion of how an event is likely to unfold and/or where the majority of its customers are likely to want to place their money. The only certainty they have is that they will structure their prices to ensure that the percentages are in their favour. Whilst there are times when various bookmakers' odds are the same on a particular event, there are many occasions when their views and, therefore, the odds they offer are very different.

These differences give rise to arbitrage opportunities and with the application of a simple mathematical model and a little search time, anyone can uncover and profit from them.

Essentially, sports-arbitrage is an activity where you place bets, at certain prices, on all possible outcomes of an event in order to secure a profit regardless of the actual result.

These opportunities occur with far more frequency than you may at first imagine (on average, 100-150 different opportunities every single day!)

but they are elusive enough to require you to undergo some learning before you will be able to find them easily.

Most arbitrage trades (arbs) will yield small profits - typically 2%-3% of capital invested. This means that if you invest £100 in an arbitrage trade of 3%, you will make a profit of about £3

This doesn't sound much at first, but with slightly larger stakes and multiple arbs per day, the profits soon add up.

What do the bookmakers think of this activity? From a business perspective bookmakers are only interested in ensuring that they generate value in every book they make. An arbitrageur's money is as good as that of any other punter and since at least half of all the bets an arbitrageur makes will lose, the bookmaker is likely to value his or her business.

There is a general misconception concerning a bookmaker's need to balance his book. It is usually believed that in an ideal book, punters would stake the amount on each possible outcome of a 'two horse race' such that the bookmaker's liability is balanced regardless of the outcome. By achieving an equal liability on both eventualities, with his margin built in, the layer is able to ensure a risk-free profit for himself.

That perception, however, does not necessarily apply to large bookmakers with plenty of working capital & lots of active clients. These companies need not be concerned with balancing their books; they merely need to attract sufficient turnover on every event. This will automatically shift the odds in their favour.

Consider this scenario in a golf 2-way match-up with 'head to head' pricing of 1.90 on each player. If the bookmaker takes a total of £10,000 on each side, he has taken £20,000 and no matter which player actually wins, he pays out only £19,000, generating a risk-free profit of £1,000.

This situation, however, describes a bookmaker's ideal scenario; it does not describe the practical reality of bookmaking. More likely would be a scenario where a total of £20,000 to win £18,000 is laid on one of the two outcomes. The other side will have attracted far less money (perhaps it is not part of an arbitrage!), with clients investing, say, a total of £10,000 to win £9,000. In this scenario, the bookmaker is exactly £8,000 'short' and he now appears to be in the position of a punter looking for a specific result. Closer inspection, however, reveals that if he gets the result he is prefers, he has won £11,000. (Keeping £20,000 and paying out £9,000). Alternatively, if the 'other side' wins, the loss is £8,000. (£18,000 having been paid with only £10,000 kept from the 'short side).

So, the bookmaker has actually risked losing £8,000 in order to win a possible £11,000 and that translates into odds of 11/8 (2.38), a 5.3% swing in his favour from the odds he quoted (1.90). Over a period of time, this added value will more than compensate for any failures to balance the book.

Nevertheless, even with this in mind, it is a fact that some bookmakers may be fundamentally opposed to clients making money from dealing with them, without incurring risk. It is, therefore, important to take measures to disguise your activities and not make it obvious that you are an arbitrageur. Later on in this book, I shall discuss various techniques that you can use in order to do this.

So it sounds easy - just find some bets, place your money and wait for the profit. What could go wrong?

Well, it can be that easy, but only when you know what you are doing. There are many pitfalls to trap novice traders and result in losses:

- Bookmaker Pricing Errors
- Bookmaker Handicap Errors
- Retirement Rules Differences
- Overtime Rules Differences
- Forgetting to bet on a Draw
- Placing the wrong bets under pressure
- Getting the stakes wrong
- Acting too slowly and missing the prices

Fortunately, all of these errors can be avoided simply by paying attention to what you are doing. The difficulty is that in the early stages most traders are very excited at the prospect of their new project and also become very nervous when placing their bets. This combination can lead to carelessness, which in turn leads to mistakes.

The best approach is to start trading with very small stakes and focus on placing as many arbs as possible. If you dedicate the first 2 or 3 months to learning the ropes without regard for making too much profit, then this will benefit you for the rest of your career as a trader.

Tools of the Trade

Computer: 2 GHz Processor, 2GB RAM 80GB HDD, Windows

Of course, it is possible to get machines with much better specifications than above but unless you have some other reasons to go higher, you can save money here by ignoring the "top-of-the-range" machines out there.

You can also use any modern Mac, and if you want to, you can run helper software that allows you to use Windows programs on your Mac

Internet connection: Broadband Internet is essential - the faster the better. A back-up dial-up account will also be useful both for emergencies and those occasions where you may require a different IP Address

Software:

Accounting: ArbAccounts* or Microsoft Money or Intuit Quicken

Communication: Email software, Skype** and ArbTalk*

Browser: ArbSurfer*

Arbitrage Notification Software: ArbAlarm*

These items are available from www.sportsarbitrageworld.com
***Many traders work in teams and ArbTalk is an excellent collaborative tool allowing chat as well as the sharing of trades. Skype is also an excellent free way to keep in touch. Coupled with a headset or mic & speakers it's also a very convenient way to call bookmakers whilst keeping your hands free to place bets online.*

Money

The most important thing for you to know at the start of your sports-arbitrage project is that your success will require a fair amount of discipline, patience and perseverance. At the beginning, things will seem overwhelming and, at times, frustrating. However, I can tell you that if you follow certain procedures and are willing to learn from your mistakes then you will find that within 3-4 months everything will seem easy and you will start to take for granted the fact that you can make £25-£100 simply by sitting at your computer and repeating the processes you have learnt.

The amount of trading capital you require to start trading will depend largely upon your goals.

> **Just starting out: Trading capital £2500 - £5,000**

Since all of your bets should be low value at this stage, £5000 is enough to allow you to place funds with 30-40 bookmakers and get the ball rolling. **Whilst your main goal at this stage should be education, you can easily double your trading capital using the risk-free bonus-hunting techniques described on page 98.**
You shouldn't be paying for any services right now, but you should be taking advantage of as many free trials as possible. Actually being able to see when and where arbs appear is a great shortcut to gaining the type of knowledge it used to take several months of trial and error to get. Visit www.sportsarbitrageworld.com and you can sign up for a free 5-day trial of ArbAlarm followed by completely free use of the software every Friday for as long as you want.

Your likely profit: £2500 from bonus-hunting followed by monthly profits of approximately £500

➢ **Part-time trading: Trading capital £10,000 - £15,000**

If you have other commitments and plan to trade for a couple of hours during the evenings and perhaps over the weekends, you'll need to increase your capital in order to ensure that the time you spend generates a worthwhile extra income. Your stakes will be larger once you are confident in your processes and it's going to be important to make sure that the periods during which you are trading are used as effectively as possible. A big part of this will be having funds on account so that you are able to execute your trades with minimum delay.

Your likely profit: £2500 from bonus-hunting followed by monthly profits of approximately £1,500

➢ **Full-time trading: £25,000 - £30,000**

This doesn't actually mean trading 8 hours a day. It really refers to the level of commitment and goals associated with your trading. At this level, you are almost certainly working from home and willing and able to trade 3 to 4 hours each day, and more during certain busy periods of the year. You should be using ArbAlarm daily and making it pay handsomely each month. **You can easily add £2500 - £5000 to your trading capital using the risk-free bonus-hunting techniques described on page 92.**

Your likely profit: £2500 from bonus-hunting followed by monthly profits of approximately £2,500 - £3500

➢ **Professional trading: £35,000 - £150,000**

At this level, sports-arbitrage and other techniques described in this book are your main occupations. 6-8 hours of trading each day - research and execution - will not be uncommon. As well as professional-level arbitrage software such as ArbAlarm, you may even have some customised trading software to assist you.

Your likely profit: £2500 from bonus-hunting followed by monthly profits of approximately £5,000 - £15,000

All of this income is, at the time of writing, tax-free in the UK.

Although you can trade from many different places in the world it is easier and cost-effective if you are able to set up bank and credit card accounts in the UK. This is because all UK bookmakers and some non-UK bookmakers allow free deposits and withdrawal from UK debit cards (and some UK credit cards). If you are not based in the UK, you might want to consider opening a UK bank account the next time you are here and then do all of your trading in British Pounds. If this is not possible, don't worry too much - all it means is that you will face slightly higher transaction costs at the start of your business. As long as you trade frequently your profits will overshadow your costs considerably.
In any case, you should set up separate accounts (bank and credit card) for your trading from your personal day-to-day accounts. Mixing arbitrage transactions with shopping bills and mortgage payments will lead to complications and possible accounting errors once your trading takes off.

You will need a bank account that will give you easy online access. You want to be able to check your balances and make transfers conveniently and doing all of this online is the most convenient way. Telephone-banking is a distant second and you should completely forget about trying to trade whilst using an account with no such facilities.

The best account to get is the one offered by Citibank because with it you get not only a Sterling-based current account but also one denominated in Euros and one denominated in US Dollars. Transfers between the different accounts are instant and are performed at very good rates of exchange.

If you cannot open an account with Citibank then try First Direct. They also offer US Dollar accounts although transfers between your Sterling and Dollar accounts will not be quite as smooth as with Citibank. However, they have exceptional customer service and very convenient online facilities.

Banks' requirements for opening accounts vary from time to time so you should check their websites for the latest terms. When you apply, don't mention that you intend to use the accounts to facilitate sports-arbitrage trading. Whilst there is nothing wrong with trading, it's usually best not to mention anything related to gambling when dealing with financial institutions!

You will also require at least one credit card. For the purposes of trading, at the time of writing, only Visa credit cards will do. Mastercard has taken a stance against gaming and you will not be able to use a Mastercard at most bookmakers.
The bank you use for your trading account will probably be able to offer you a credit card as well. Take them up on this with as high a credit limit as they will give you. It is useful to have at least one spare credit card but most traders have a collection of 3 or more. You may not use them often but it's better to have them available than to be left high and dry in the middle of a trading scenario.

In addition to a bank account and credit card, you will require accounts with a number of online wallets. These are accounts into which you can place deposits and which will act as a 'central holding account' for a number of bookmakers. The largest and most widely-used online wallets are currently www.neteller.com and www.moneybookers.com and I recommend that you set up accounts with each of them.

If you have downloaded ArbSurfer (either the Preview or pro version will do), then you should do the following:

For banks and/or credit card companies:

a) In ArbSurfer, open the Sites Repository & press the 'Enable Filtering' button at the bottom.
b) Press the + button to add a filter & set it as Categories Contains Bank & Press OK
c) The Repository will now display a list of banks & credit card companies.
d) Simply double-click on the ones you want to open and navigate to the sign-up forms.

For Online Wallets:

a) In ArbSurfer, open the Sites Repository & press the 'Enable Filtering' button at the bottom.
b) Press the + button to add a filter & set it as Categories Contains Wallet & Press OK
c) The Repository will now display a list of online wallets.
d) Simply double-click on the ones you want to open and navigate to the sign-up forms.

If you filled out your Profile then ArbSurfer will fill the forms out for you and all you will need to do is add any missing information and submit the form.

Make a note of the usernames & passwords required to log into the accounts you have set up. You should then go to each site and log in for the first time. When you do this, ArbSurfer will prompt you to save the codes and if you click YES then these codes will be encrypted and stored securely in ArbSurfer so that the next time you visit the site you can be logged in automatically. You can download ArbSurfer from www.arbsurfer.com

Bookmakers

Before you can begin to trade, you will need to set up accounts with a large number of bookmakers. It is a very good idea to set up your accounts well before you start to trade – attempting to set up accounts as and when you need them will result in a lot of wasted time and opportunities for you later on.

A list of the most useful bookmakers is provided on the following website:

www.bookmakerreviews.com

In most cases, you will be able to open accounts without depositing any funds. This is advantageous as it allows you to make your preparations even if your trading capital is not yet fully at your disposal.

Setting up such a large number of accounts can be a daunting and time-consuming task; fortunately, ArbSurfer automates the endless form-filling thus speeding up this process considerably.

Once you have downloaded and installed the software, you will be taken through a set-up wizard. Follow this through and set up a Profile. After this, you can use the links provided in the software to visit each bookmaker site's sign-up page and the software will automatically fill out the forms with the data you have provided in your Profile. In some cases, you may be required to type in a verification code or other data not contained within the Profile, and then you simply submit the form.

Some of the bookmakers will set up your account with the username and password combination you placed in your Profile. Others will assign random log-in codes for you and email them to you. In any case, whenever you set up a new bookmaker account, take the time to write down the bookmaker's address and the log-in codes so that you have a record of them. The Pro version of ArbSurfer will remember all of your codes for you and even log you into the sites automatically when you visit them.

As you set up your accounts, a question about how to spread your funds amongst them will come to mind. Do you keep the money in the bank and wait for an arbitrage opportunity to arise before making a transfer or do you put the money with the bookmakers in anticipation? This usually seems like a catch-22 situation to new traders. If you don't have your money ready at the bookmakers, then you waste too much time making the deposit when a trade appears and miss the prices when you need to bet. But if you start putting your money with the bookmakers, it gets spread thinly and you still may get an arbitrage opportunity with a bookmaker where you don't have enough funds. . .

The solution is to combine the approaches intelligently and place funds with bookmakers **selectively**. I suggest the following approach:

1. Select the bookmakers you will use. The list provided on the site below is a good starting point

www.bookmakerreviews.com

2. Provide the bookmakers with all required documentation in advance. For example, in order to make your first deposit with an Australian bookmaker you will need to send them a fax or scan of your ID and credit card. If you do not do this in advance, the process will seriously hinder your ability to successfully place a bet with them on the first occasion that they are involved in a sports-arbitrage trade. Look through the sites you plan to use and see which ones require more information from you.

3. Some bookmakers provide Instant-Bet accounts that will debit your card automatically at the time you place a bet. Any accounts that offer

Instant-Bet facilities can immediately be taken off your short-list of accounts that require advanced funding.

4. Look for bookmakers that will accept deposits via your online wallet at www.neteller.com. Deposits via Neteller is usually instant – this means that you can keep a large central balance in your Neteller account ready to be used with any of the bookmakers rather than holding smaller individual balances at the bookmakers themselves.

5. Decide which accounts are going to be used most frequently: This is obviously quite difficult because it seems to require a lot of foresight. However, the data provided at Sports Arbitrage World now makes this task much simpler.

www.sportsarbitrageworld.com/previousresults/index.htm

This page processes a very large database of expired arbs and displays exactly which bookmakers were involved heavily with which sports during any given time-period. This is an extremely useful tool, which you will probably refer back to frequently as it gives you a great idea of where money needs to be placed each month.

Following steps 1-5, you will produce two lists - accounts which need advanced funding and accounts that do not.

In common with many activities that seem complex, sports-arbitrage trading can be simplified by considering & mastering the individual actions that make up the entire process. Avoid the mistake of assuming that it will be better to pick things up as you go along instead of investing some time beforehand to really think about what's involved. In most cases, the people who fail at sports-arbitrage for various reasons are people who ignored the inherent folly of going live on their trading project without sufficient preparation.

Preparation & Organisation are the two main factors that will determine your success or failure.

Before you begin trading, having chosen your bookmaker accounts and decided how they will be funded, the next step is to familiarise yourself with the bookmaker sites. Place a few 10 pence bets at the sites that confuse you. Make sure that you fully understand how to place bets at the sites you will be using. If you place 50 bets of 10 pence each, you will have a thorough understanding of the way the bookmaker sites work and the most it will have cost you is £5. This small investment will pay dividends later on when you are trading under pressure.

Managing Bookmaker Accounts

One of the most important defensive aspects of sports-arbitrage trading is protecting your bookmaker accounts so that you postpone and/or completely avoid situations where bookmakers either severely limit your stakes or close your accounts.

Many novice traders ignore this issue and jump into trading without taking any precautions. As a result, they find their accounts limited within weeks and subsequently write-off sports-arbitrage as "..impossible to do for any length of time because of stake limits".

Some of the common-sense precautions that every trader should take are:

- ✓ **Avoid betting on prices which are clearly bookmaker errors**. If you are unsure whether or not the price is an error, you should err towards caution as this will also reduce your own risk of bets being voided under the Palpable Error rule.
- ✓ **Bet in round sums**. Round up or down to the nearest £5 and never bet in pence e.g. £10.72
- ✓

- ✓ **Don't bet the maximum stake.** This will mark you out as a trader almost immediately
- ✓ **Never withdraw your full balance.** Unless you want to close the account down. It's okay to withdraw some of your funds and 50% - 60% is probably a good proportion. The problem is that withdrawing your entire balance will attract the bookmaker's attention (especially if it is a large amount) and it can indicate that you are a trader who is running short of liquidity.
- ✓ **When emailing or phoning bookmakers, under no circumstances should you mention arbs, middles, exchanges or anything else related to trading**

- ✓ **Know what you are betting on.** If you need to call to place a bet, make sure that you know exactly what you are betting on and how to pronounce the team/player's name (only a trader would call to place a bet on a team or player he or she is completely unfamiliar with)

These steps will give you the appearance of a Mug Punter - the bookmakers' favourite type of customer.

You should also use the accumulator betting techniques, discussed later in this book, to place risk-free doubles and trebles with bookmakers whenever the opportunity arises. This will definitely make you look like a mug because it will be impossible for the bookmaker to know what you are really doing.

Multiple Accounts

If you have friends or family who will allow you to open and run bookmaker accounts in their names, this gives you extra opportunities whenever you do get limited on one of your own accounts. However, multiple accounts are not a substitute for the precautions listed on the previous page - it does not matter how many accounts you have access to if you do not know how to look after them.

There are a few different options when it comes to holding multiple accounts. Eventually you will probably need to use them all but there is probably no need to rush into all of them at once.

These general rules apply whenever you open multiple accounts as they help to disguise your tactics from the bookmakers:

- ✓ Use a different credit card for each extra account you have with a bookmaker. This is obvious if the account is in the name of a friend or relative because it will have to be a card in their name but the rule applies when you open a telephone account and an internet-based account with the same bookmaker.
- ✓ If your spouse or partner can use a maiden name for extra accounts then use this advantage
- ✓ If you have an alternate address you can provide then use this when opening the extra accounts
- ✓ Delete your cookies regularly. Some browsers can be set to do this for you automatically and this is a good option as it is easy to forget.
- ✓ Disconnect from and reconnect to the Internet regularly. This changes your IP address.
- ✓ Try to avoid using your multiple accounts simply to increase the amount you can stake on the arbs you do. This will just result in all accounts becoming limited at similar times and it also increases the chance for losses if prices slip away as you try to put all of the extra bets on. The point of your multiple accounts is to enhance the longevity of your trading, not short-term profits.

Open telephone accounts

Many of the UK bookmakers offer telephone accounts. Some of these are run as completely separate accounts from the internet-based accounts and this can prove to be quite an advantage. Try Bet 365, Blue Square, Ladbrokes, Skybet, Totexpress, William Hill

Often you will find that larger stakes are accepted by phone than by web. But try not to get too greedy or you will attract attention and get limited.

Use the local betting shops

If you are based in the UK then you can place some of your bets in the shops run by Coral, Ladbrokes and William Hill. This is best suited to exchange-traded soccer arbs

Open Internet accounts in different names

You will need permission from a friend or relative to open accounts in their names. You will use their details - name, address, and credit card information - so there needs to be a very high degree of trust

Mark Dawson adds:

"I do operate with multiple accounts. Some books are cleverer at spotting this than others. I moved house 2 years ago and have most of my books registered at my old address, I also have a credit card in my wife's maiden name, which means I can sign up using a different name at a different address. In addition to on line accounts, I have telephone accounts at Hills, Totexpress, Blue square, and others, where I have used the same address as on line, and to my knowledge they have not noticed, although I have used a different credit/debit card. I have been sussed as having 2 (multiple) accounts by b365, and my limit is £10 on just about everything, my accounts with b365 are linked together, so if I bet £10 on one a/c my max on the other a/c is £0. There are 2 ways they (the bookies) find out about multiple accounts.

1) The IP address. If you are on broadband the ISP address remains the same for 6 to 8 weeks at a time if you enter a website using the same computer, they will pick up on it. You can resolve this either by using separate Internet connections or proxy services.

2) Cookies. Delete the cookies every time before you enter the site, or else they will pick up on it being the same person. Unfortunately, restrictions are an occupational hazard.

Theory

There are a number of different formulae you will use as you introduce more complex trading techniques to your armoury. However, the most fundamental one is that which shows you how to determine whether or not an arbitrage situation exists in a given event.

Bookmakers express their prices (or odds) in several ways. Each format represents the same information, i.e. how much you will win if you bet on an outcome, but the formats are different enough to cause confusion to those who do not understand them properly.

Odds (sometimes called prices) are numbers used to calculate how much money you will win with your stake on a certain event. The general rule is that the higher the odds for a given outcome the lower the probability of that outcome.

Odds are actually just probability percentages converted into numbers. As an arbitrage trader, you will, in fact, be more interested in the probability percentages but in order to trade effectively you must understand how to interpret the prices in their various formats.

Three formats of odds are widely used.

European (decimal) | British (fractions) | American (moneyline)

Some bookmakers support more than one format and conversion between formats is possible.

Here is example of how odds are presented in different formats:

UK-format prices are fractional, for example, 6/4 (six-to-four)

EU-format prices are decimal, for example, 2.50

US-style prices are numerical, for example, +250

All of the above example prices, 6/4, 2.50 and +250 express exactly the same price!

Now let's make some calculations to better explain the odds formats. It is important to distinguish between 'payout' and 'win'. 'Payout' refers to the sum of the amount of money won together with stake. 'Win' refers to the amount of real money won (i.e. 'Payout' minus the stake).

We will use an example stake of £100

European Odds (decimal)

Calculate payout by multiplying the stake with the odds offered. The odds show how many units the bookmaker pays out for one unit staked. European odds show us the total amount of money we win together with our stake. In this case it's £100 x 2.50 = £250

British Odds (fractions)

British odds show winnings, or how much money you win minus your stake. £200 x 6/4 = £150. By betting £100 on the event, a win results in an extra £150 coming back to you i.e. the payout is £250

American Odds (Moneyline)

The easiest way to understand a moneyline is to think of it as an indication of the amount you need to bet to win $100 (or 100 of whatever currency you are betting in) or the amount you will win if you bet $100.

Moneylines are expressed with a negative number, e.g. -110, or a positive number, such as +120. A negative money line number indicates what you must wager to win $100, and a positive money line number indicates what you will win if you risk $100.

If you bet $110 on a team with a money line of -110 and they win, you will win $100 (plus return of your original $110 bet). If you bet $100 on a team with a money line of +120, and they win, you will win $120 (plus return of the original $100 bet). Unlike point spread bets, the teams do not have to win by any particular number of points.

You do not have to bet an amount equal to the moneyline number. You can bet more or less and the payoff simply becomes a proportion of this amount. For example, if you bet $11 on a money line of -110 and your bet wins, you will win $10. If you bet $50 on a moneyline of +120 and your selection is correct, you will win $60.

Converting American style odds to European odds and vice versa

To convert American odds to European, simply divide an underdog's price (positive odds) by 100 and add 1, or divide the favourite's price (negative odds) into 100 (after dropping the minus-sign) and add 1.

To convert European odds of less than 2.0 to American, subtract 1 and divide into -100. For odds greater than 2.0, subtract 1 and multiply by 100.

Examples:

1. Positive Odds:

Moneyline: +150

Divide positive odds by 100 and add 1 =>

150/100 + 1 = 2.50

To illustrate this in reverse:

EU Odds: 2.50

For odds greater than 2.0, subtract 1 and multiply by 100. =>

(2.50 - 1) x 100 = +150

2. Negative Odds:

EU odds: 1.40

This is under 2.00 so we subtract 1 and divide into 100:

100 / (1.40 - 1) = -250 i.e. the moneyline is -250

To illustrate this in reverse:

Moneyline: -250

This is negative so we divide the negative odds into 100 (after dropping the minus-sign) and add 1:

100/250 + 1 = 0.40 + 1 = 1.40

Converting UK-style odds to EU-style is straightforward. Simply convert the UK fraction into a decimal and add 1:

UK odds: 6/4

convert the UK fraction into a decimal and add 1 =>

1.50 + 1 = 2.50

To convert an EU price into a UK price, minus 1 and convert the result into a fraction:

EU odds: 2.50

minus 1 and convert the result into a fraction =>

2.50 − 1 = 1.50 = 3/2 = 6/4

Now that you understand what the prices mean in terms of stakes and payouts, let's apply this to sports-arbitrage.

The essence of sports-arbitrage is that when the prices allow, a trader can bet on all outcomes in an event and generate a total payout greater than the total staked.

The method used to identify whether or not a set of prices allow for an arbitrage trade to take place is to convert the prices into percentages and then sum those percentages. A sum total less than 100% indicates an arbitrage trade.

In order to convert prices into percentages these days, most traders will use some form of specialised calculator or spreadsheet. However, it is worth understanding the formulae behind these tools; with this understanding many traders begin to develop the ability to recognise potential arbitrage trades on sight alone. This can be a formidable tool in itself when browsing bookmaker sites but the real value is that it translates into an ability to recognise when a change in price results in the expiration of an arbitrage trade.

However, if the following 4 pages don't make much sense to you, don't worry! Most of the arbitrage tools you will go on to use will incorporate automatic calculation of arbitrage percentages and stake apportionment. If the mathematics behind this doesn't interest you, please skip ahead now to page 30.

Since EU-style odds are predominant amongst bookmakers, the convention is to use this format and, where odds are presented differently, to convert them into EU-format before continuing.

In order to convert an EU price into a percentage, simply divide the price into 100.

Examples:

1.20 => 100/1.20 = 83.33%
2.50 => 100/2.50 = 40%

Let's look at an example of a pair of prices that create an arbitrage situation:

Player 1: 1.20

Player 2: 8.00

To determine whether an arbitrage exists, we convert each price to a percentage and then sum these percentages. If the sum is less than 100%, an arbitrage exists:

1.20 => 100/1.20 = 83.33%
8.00 => 100/8.00 = 12.50%

SUM = 95.83%

The sum is less than 100% so an arbitrage exists.

The significance of the sum total of the individual percentages is that if you were to invest this amount of Pounds into the trade, your payout would be £100. In this example, a total investment of £95.83 would yield a payout of £100 i.e. a profit of £4.17

The Return on Investment (ROI) of this trade is calculated as:

4.17/95.83 x 100 = 4.35%

When you have summed the arbitrage percentage, as shown on the previous page, you may go on to calculate

1. the size of the payout/profit from any given total stake (e.g. Total Stake = £1000)

Payout = (Total Stake / Percentage Sum) = (1000 / 95.833) = £1043.48

Profit = = (Total Stake / Percentage Sum) - Total Stake = (1000 / 95.833) - 1000 = £1043.48 - £1000 = £43.48

2. the size of total stake required in order to generate a desired payout/profit (e.g. Desired Payout = £1000)

Total Stake = Desired Payout/Percentage Sum = 1000/95.833 = £958.33

Profit = Desired Payout - Total Stake = 1000 - 958.33 = 41.67

In order to calculate the component stakes that make up the trade, we divide each individual bet percentage by the percentage sum and then multiply this result by the desired total investment. For example, if we stay with the above bets and assume that we want to stake a total of £1000 in this trade, the calculations follow:

Player 1: 1.20 => 100/1.20 = 83.33%
Player 2: 8.00 => 100/8.00 = 12.50%

        SUM = 95.83%

Total Stake = £1000

Stake on Player 1 = (83.33 / 95.833) x 1000 = £869.56
Stake on Player 2 = (12.50 / 95.833) x 1000 = £130.44

The same methodology can be extended to arbitrage trades with 3 or more outcomes. For example, a trade generated by a soccer match may have 3 outcomes: Team 1, Team 2 and Draw

Example:

Team 1:   1.30

Team 2:   7.00

Draw: 17.00

The percentage sum of this trade is calculated by dividing each price into 100 & summing the total:

Team 1:   1.30   =>   100/1.30   = 76.92%

Team 2:   7.00   =>   100/7.00   = 14.29%

Draw: 17.00   =>   100/17.00   = 5.88%

                                    SUM = 97.09

The individual stake for each bet is calculated by dividing each individual bet percentage by the percentage sum and then multiplying this result by the desired total investment:

Team 1:   76.92 / 97.09 x 1000   = £792.25

Team 2:   14.29 / 97.09 x 1000   = £147.19

Draw: 5.88 / 97.09 x 1000   = £ 60.56

In the practical reality of day-to-day trading, you will probably never make such calculations manually as most sports-arbitrage software will perform these operations for you automatically.

Accounting

Keeping detailed accounts will contribute to your continued success as a sports-arbitrage trader. It will serve you well to form the habit at the very start. The best way is to set up a system to enable you to do this conveniently. Remember, as a reasonably active sports-arbitrage trader you will easily find yourself involved in at least 100 separate transactions every week.

Apart from the obvious issue of the importance of knowing your profit and loss, keeping up-to-date accounts will allow you to know in moments exactly where your money is at any time. This is critical to efficient trading. It only takes a week of inaction due to funds being in the wrong place to turn a promising month into a below average month of profits.

It's also important because unless you check your wins, deposits and withdrawals, you're leaving it to the bookmakers to get it right every time. They do make mistakes and if you are not on-the-ball the mistakes will, more often than not, cost you money.

Suggested tools:

Although spreadsheets can be very useful for tracking trades, unless you have some fairly decent programming skills, they become unwieldy as your activity grows and your records accumulate.

A purpose-built solution is available from this website:

www.arbaccounts.com

This provides a seamless trade-calculation, input and record-keeping experience. However, you may prefer to use accounts software which you already own; for example, Intuit Quicken or Microsoft Money. Although these programs are not specifically designed for sports-arbitrage trading, it's fairly easy to set them up so that they cover everything. An additional benefit is that they also provide a number of pre-configured reports, which can tell you your profit & loss over different periods, your accounts transactions & balances etc.

In this chapter, I'm going to describe exactly how to set up MS Money to track your trading accounts. The first step, however, is for you to gather ALL of your information together. You need the following information:

Bank Accounts:

- ✓ Banks' contact details- internet access details (web address plus log-in codes)
- ✓ account number, sort code
- ✓ account balance
- ✓ overdraft limit

Credit & Debit Cards:

- ✓ Issuers' contact details
- ✓ internet access details (web address plus log-in codes)
- ✓ card number
- ✓ card security number
- ✓ balance
- ✓ credit limit
- ✓ cashback/loyalty points awards program details

Moneybookers, Neteller, PayPal, Firepay and other online wallets:

- ✓ Issuers' contact details
- ✓ internet access details (web address plus log-in codes)
- ✓ account currency
- ✓ account balance

Bookmaker Accounts:

- ✓ Bookmakers' contact details
- ✓ internet access details (web address plus log-in codes)
- ✓ account currency
- ✓ account balance

Once you have entered all of this information into your accounts program, you will have a one-stop-shop for everything and this in itself will help you to stay organised.

Once you have your details ready, start up the program. The software will take you through a wizard so that you may easily set up all of your accounts.

Bank Accounts

These should be set up as bank accounts - the process is straight-forward and you will have an opportunity to enter all of the information that you have gathered about your accounts.

Credit & Debit Cards

These should be set up as credit or debit cards - again the process is straight-forward and you will have an opportunity to enter all of the information that you have gathered about your accounts.

Neteller & other accounts

These should be set up as bank accounts.

Bookmaker Accounts

These should be set up as bank accounts.

Pending Wins

This is a special account which you should set up as a bank account. You will use this account to list any wins which you are expecting but which have not yet been paid. I'll explain this in more detail later on in this chapter.

Transactions

Once your accounts are set up, you need to think about the transactions which will take place between them. MS Money allows 3 basic types of transaction: Transfers, deposits & withdrawals.

We will use each type of transaction for specific purposes:

Transfers: movement of funds between accounts

Withdrawals: bets you place

Deposits: winnings from bets

Transfers

When you move money from one account to another, this is a transfer. So, if you were sending money from a bank account to a bookmaker account, this would be a transfer. Other examples of transfers:

> Credit card account to bookmaker account (i.e. when you wish to fund a bookmaker account using your credit card
> Bank account to credit card account (i.e. when you pay your credit card bill at the end of the month with funds from your bank account)
> Bookmaker to credit card account (i.e. when you withdraw funds from a bookmaker and he pays it back to your credit card)

Withdrawals

Whenever you place a bet at a bookmaker you record this as a withdrawal. Think of it this way: you have some money on your bookmaker account and you are going to spend some of it on a bet. When you enter the bet you will also categorise it - more details on categories are below.

Deposits

Whenever a bet wins, this will be recorded as a deposit on that particular account. You will also categorise these transactions as described below.

Categories

A useful feature of MS Money is that you can categorise each transaction. Normally this would be used to tie up expenses so you could see where your money goes. For example, you may spend £25 at Tesco and categorise this as "Groceries". Later in the week, you may then go to the corner shop to pick up some milk and eggs. You spend £1.50 on this and also categorise it as "Groceries". Then if you were to check your MS Money reports, you would be able to see that you spent a total of £26.50 on Groceries even though it was at different shops and at different times.

We're going to use these categories in a slightly different way so that instead of seeing how much we spend on Groceries, we will be able to see how much we spent on a particular arbitrage trade and how much we won on it. We'll have all of the bets and wins categorised as the same arbitrage trade, which means that we will be able to tie up all parts of an arbitrage trade together even though they were transacted on different accounts.

I would suggest setting up your categories in the following format:

Month : SportName - ArbNumber

e.g.: June: Tennis-001 June: Golf-003 June: Golf-004 etc

Pending Wins

This account will list the *expected wins* from any trades that have not yet settled. Once the trade has settled and you know exactly which account the win should go to, you can transfer the whole transaction from the PendingWins account into the correct bookmaker account.

An example

Consider an arbitrage trade in tennis - your first tennis trade in June - with Roddick @ 2.10 at Pinnacle Sports and Federer @ 2.00 at Olympic Sportsbook. Let's say that you're investing a total of £1000 on the trade and you do not have any money deposited at either bookmaker. I'll describe each individual action you will take, whilst describing how it will be recorded in your accounts software:

You need to bet £488 at Pinnacle and £512 at Olympic:

Action: Use your credit card to deposit £488 at Pinnacle Sports **Record:** Transfer: £488 Credit Card Account to Pinnacle Sports Account Category: Tennis: June001

Action: Use your credit card to deposit £512 at Olympic Sportsbook **Record:** Transfer: £512 Credit Card Account to Olympic Sportsbook Account Category: Tennis: June001

Action: Bet £488 on Roddick at Pinnacle Sports **Record:** **Withdraw/Spend** £488 from Pinnacle Sports Account Category: Tennis: June001

Action: Bet £512 on Federer at Olympic Sportsbook **Record:** **Withdraw/Spend** £512 from Olympic Sportsbook Account Category: Tennis: June001

Action: You now stand to win either £1024.80 from Pinnacle if Roddick wins or £1024.00 from Olympic if Federer wins. **Record:** Deposit £1024 to Pending Wins (always list the lowest possible

win - if the higher one comes in than you can change it at that time)
Category: Tennis: June001

Action: 24 hours later, Roddick wins the match and you receive £1024.80 in your Pinnacle bookmaker account **Record:** Delete the deposit from Pending Wins & enter a new deposit into your Pinnacle Sports Account of £1024.80 Category: Tennis: June001 (Instead of deleting the transaction from Pending Wins, you can cut & paste it from Pending Wins to the Pinnacle Sports Account)

This process is to be repeated with all arbs that you place. At any time, you will be able to go to your reports and check to see the profits on any category. This way you can see your overall profits, or just the profits you have made on a single sport or even how much profit you are waiting for on arbs that have yet to settle.

Finding Suitable Trades

There are two ways to find suitable trades: use software to scan the markets automatically and inform you in real-time or locate the trades manually. Whilst most traders will primarily rely upon software, it can pay healthy dividends to use a hybrid approach – using software to do the legwork on the majority of trades and using more sophisticated knowledge-based techniques to find other trades manually.

In any case, you should download ArbAlarm software from the site below and experience a free trial to get an idea of the frequency with which suitable trades appear.

www.arbalarm.com

In a later chapter, I shall talk more about this sports-arbitrage software and how to optimise your profits whilst using it. The rest of this chapter, however, is devoted to describing the basic techniques used to find arbs in the following sports:

- Boxing
- Cricket
- Darts
- Football
- Golf
- Motor racing
- Rugby
- Tennis
- Baseball
- Ice Hockey

Boxing

Boxing matches may be priced up with 2-outcomes or 3-outcomes:

Fighter 1 - Fighter 2 or

Fighter 1 - Tie - Fighter 2

It is usually US-orientated bookmakers who use the 2-outcome model and UK/European which include the Tie.

Standard arbs can be found by comparing like with like but there is also an advanced technique which can be used to combine 2 and 3 outcome bets to uncover arbs which are invisible to most traders.

Mark Dawson explains:

"...It took a while for me to suss this out but when I did it was a "Eureka" moment for sure. A lot of the time when you're looking for arbs in boxing, you'll often find them between bookmakers that include the Tie against those which do not. These appear risky because you could end up losing both bets if there is a Tie so, of course, you have to bet on the Tie as well. Sometimes this ends up increasing the percentages to the point that there is no trade..."

An example

BOOKMAKER	FIGHTER 1	FIGHTER 2	TIE
PINNACLE SPORTS	1.75	2.00	
WILLIAM HILL	1.50	2.50	26.00

"Taking Pinnacle Sports' 1.73 on Fighter 1, William Hill's 2.50 on Fighter 2 and the Tie at 26.00 creates an overall percentage of 100.99% i.e. no arbitrage trade"(see page 27 for an explanation of the calculations involved to determine the overall percentage)

"...but the really good stuff happens when you look a little beyond the obvious. What you've got to remember is that the bookmaker that doesn't include the Tie will refund your stake money if the fight ends in a Tie. What is means is that you only have to cover one losing bet with a hedge on the Tie. Keeping this little fact in mind suddenly turns all of those near-arbitrage trades into actual arbitrage trades"

An example

BOOKMAKER	FIGHTER 1	FIGHTER 2	TIE
PINNACLE SPORTS	1.75	2.00	
WILLIAM HILL	1.50	2.50	26.00

	STAKES	PAYOUT	PROFIT
FIGHTER 1	565.83	**990.21**	11.89
FIGHTER 2	396.08	**990.21**	11.89
TIE	16.40	426.40+565.83=**992.23**	13.91
TOTAL STAKES	**978.32**		

Cricket

Standard arbs can be found in cricket by searching the main UK bookmakers early for domestic matches. Arbs on international matches require you to broaden your search to include Australian and European bookmakers. High value opportunities in cricket can be taken advantage of by using the betting-in-running markets. Patrick Goodman explains some of the techniques he uses to exploit arbs as large as 20% in this sport:

"Basically what I'm looking for are sudden changes in a match which will force the bookmakers to change their prices. When this happens, you get arbs either between the sharp bookmakers and the ones who haven't moved their prices at all or between companies who have taken different views on the change. The range of possibilities is fairly broad so it helps if you've got an interest in the sport. For example, I'll check prices following the coin toss, a change in weather, an injury or a change in the batting order. The coin toss makes a big difference if the match is going to be played into the night as it forces one team to bat without sunlight. Not every bookie is going to take this fully into account."

I myself have had some excellent results following the market known as "Next Man Out" during matches I watch live on TV. Bookmakers price up who they think will be the next batsman to fall and they create some excellent arbs between themselves when the batsmen are fairly evenly matched because they seem to start pricing up according to opinions more than anything else. When the two batsmen are very different in their skill levels, prices tend to chop and change quite a bit and this also provide some good opportunities. You will see that the prices move as runs are scored and the receiving batsman changes. Usually the better player is assumed to be more likely to stay in but, since he will be the one who is probably batting more often and more aggressively, he ends up taking far more risks and this isn't always expressed in the prices.

Simon Ferguson uses cricket to bet on middles:

"I use the Total Runs markets quite a bit. You don't always get a decent trade but there will often be at least a couple of decent middles up for grabs..."

Middles are explained in detail later in this book but here is a quick example of what you may find when looking for these bets in cricket:

Bookmaker (x)

Team A to Score 210 runs or under: 1.65 61.90%

Team A to Score over 210 runs: 2.20 45.45%

At the same time over at Bookmaker (y)

Team A to Score 220 runs or under: 1.91 52.38%

Team A to Score over 220 runs 1.91 52.38%

Just looking at the above figures you'll see a 2% guaranteed profit between betting over 210 runs with bookie (x) and 220 runs or under at bookie (y). In addition, if the team's final score is between 211 and 220 both of your bets win in full.

"...more often than not, these middles won't be combined with an arbitrage trade - there will be a total percentage of maybe 101% which locks in a small loss if the middle doesn't land. I usually take any middle up to 102%. Other small arbs make up for the small losses and whenever middle lands it boosts the profits very nicely."

Darts

There are relatively few darts events each year but they can be profitable if approached correctly. As well as normal match-betting there are two markets unique to darts, which provide arbs often yielding double-figure percentages. They are the "9-Dart Finish" and "Number of 180's" markets. The former is a 2-way market, usually expressed as "Will there be a 9-Dart Finish - Yes/No". The latter may be expressed by some bookmakers as a 2-way under/over market or as a 3-way market offering bands of values. As long as you have all values covered, you can combine bets from the 2-way markets with those from the 3-way markets.

Betting in-running is also a profitable trading strategy with darts as Mark Dawson explains:

"As with any betting in-running situation, you're looking for events which potentially have a big impact on the result. I like trading darts in-running because of the quick maths involved. You've got to keep in mind what the player needs to score and if he misses a throw you've got to quickly work out how much more difficult it makes it for him to win. For example, if a player needs to score 142 to win he could do it in 3 darts. This is going to lengthen the odds on his opponent as he is effectively just waiting to be beaten. If the thrower gets a double-ten followed by a mis-throw which lands in single-six you know that he suddenly has no chance of winning with the next dart and that's the time to bet on any left over long prices on his opponent. I've had 25%-30% arbs 3 or 4 times in single matches doing this. It can also be quite interesting watching how much the players are drinking as that can have a major impact on their play – if I see a player that looks worse for wear I may take a small risk and bet on his opponent in anticipation of a balls up!"

Football

During the football season there are often over 500 matches which take place around the world each week. Multiply this by the number of bookmakers and the thought of finding arbs in soccer can become very quickly overwhelming. Andy Summervale is a specialist in football and describes some of the techniques he uses:

"I chose soccer as my specialty because I love the game and the markets offered are by far the widest and deepest. The sheer number of matches creates the opportunity but also make it almost impossible to trade effectively without the help of some sort of software to work through all of the regular home-away-draw match bets. But the trick is to look beyond these markets and venture into cards, correct scores/under-over bets and Asian handicaps.

Many of my arbs come from the subscription service I use, but I also work in a group of traders and we share our manual finds - almost all on soccer. After a while you get to know the lines and the bookmakers who will provide the trades. You have to serve an apprenticeship if you want to be a manual trader. It's hard at first and I can well remember long weekends looking and finding not a lot. There are great opportunities in football trading because there are so many markets priced up. Many arbs can be found if you look one step beyond the obvious and they stay around for a while. I have seen reasonably obvious 5%ers on Premiership games hang around for 24 hours for example.

Traditionally arbitrageurs will try and close out a trade as quickly as possible to make sure the prices don't move against them - textbook stuff. When you have more experience of the prices within a sport you may not necessarily do that. It is common for me to pick up leg 1 on Tuesday, leg 2 on Friday and leg 3 on Saturday. I have learned to spot when a price is really good, and I know that I can at least get out roughly even if I can't make an arbitrage profit on it. On Saturday if you had access to the best price on every line which had been offered that week it would be easy to trade. However the best prices get snapped up during the week. A large part of my success at present results from knowing which prices to put into my pocket for the weekend"

Andy also uses a very imaginative arbitrage technique with accumulator bets, described in detail over here

"Back to cards, correct scores/under-over bets and Asian handicaps: the first two often throw up both arbitrage trades and middles, whilst the Asians are so poorly understood by the majority that the profits are easy pickings. The cards market is where bookies offer you odds on predicting the number of yellow and red cards produced in a match. Bookmakers award 10 points for every yellow card and 25 points for every red card. When a player receives a yellow, followed by a second yellow then an immediate red, the score is 35 points as only the first yellow and red are counted for scoring.

The bookies format their markets in one of a few ways, which I'll explain below.

Format One – Exact Middle

Bet on Under 30 Points

Bet on Exactly 30 Points

Bet on Over 30 Points

Bookmakers that offer this market usually price up around even money for each side of the "exact middle" number.

Format Two – Varied Point Middle

Bet on Under 21

Bet on 21 – 46

Bet on Over 46

Bet on Under 21 covers me for one or two yellow cards whilst the Middle Bet, Bet on 21 – 46 covers me for a score of 25, 30, 35, 40 and 45. It's this middle ground that can prove a starting point for arbitrage trades, especially when the bookie is too high or too low on his predictions for the total match score.

Format Three – Individual Pricing

Bet on 61+

Bet on 51-60

Bet on 41-50

Bet on 31-40

Bet on 21-30

Bet on 11-20

Bet on 0-10

Only a small number of bookmakers use format but it gives me the ability to mix and match with markets two and three at the other bookmakers.

Arbitrage trades and middles can be had by mixing pretty much any combination of the 3 formats.

Combining Formats One & Two:

Bookmaker 1

Bet on Under 30 1.91

Bet on Exactly 30 6.00

Bet on Over 30 2.20

Bookmaker 2

Bet on Under 35 2.00

Bet on 35-50 2.50

Bet on Over 50 4.00

A bet on Over 30 at Bookie 1 combined with Under 35 at Bookie 2 covers all outcomes and using the above prices creates an arb of over 4.75%.

Combining Formats Two & Three:

Bookmaker 1

Bet on Under 41 2.00

Bet on 41-50 5.00

Bet on Over 50 2.80

Bookmaker 2

Bet on 61+ 5.00

Bet on 51-60 9.00

Bet on 41-50 8.00

Bet on 31-40 7.00

Bet on 21-30 6.50

Bet on 11-20 7.00

Bet on 0-10 13.00

A bet on Under 41 at Bookie 1 combined with 3 bets at Bookie 2 (41-50, 51-60 and 61+) creates an arbitrage trade of a little over 6%

Combining Format 2 at different bookmakers:

Bookmaker 1

Bet on Over 60 4.50

Bet on 45 –60 2.50

Bet on Under 45 1.91 (52.38%)

Bookmaker 2

Bet on Over 40 2.25 (44.44%)

Bet on 25-40 2.75

Bet on Under 25 3.00

Bet Under 45 at Bookie 1 and Over 40 at Bookie 2 for a 3% arb

I use similar techniques in the Under/Over goals markets where some bookies give you under/over 2.5 and others offer 3-way markets with an exact middle, for example,

2 or under

exactly 2

3 and above

Asian handicap markets offer some great trading opportunities, both between the bookies themselves and with the exchanges

It's a very good idea to open an account with www.seangraham.com for soccer. This is a large bookmaker based in Northern Ireland. Their prices on soccer handicaps always throw up a lot of good-sized arbs. They are usually quite slow to update their prices and their Total Goals prices are also worth checking out. They payout efficiently but they will hit you with a £25 limit after a few bets. I was able to last 6 months with them and made almost £16,000 using just their soccer prices in arbs against other bookmakers and exchanges.

I also suggest that if you are in the UK, you think about using bookmaker shops for soccer prices. Their coupons come out early in the week and usually have a selection of high prices which can be laid off at the exchanges or traded against other online bookies. Offline, I use Corals, Ladbrokes & William Hill. I keep my bets below £500 to avoid attention when I win in this shop and I try to make the managers my friends. Always ask the counter clerk to phone their head office to confirm that the price on the coupon is what you will get on your bet - this is important as they sometimes update their prices on their screens but obviously not on the coupons which are printed out."

Golf

There are a number of reasons that golf is such an excellent sport for arbitrage.

- ✓ There are at least 2 tournaments every week for 10 months of the year
- ✓ There are 4 Majors each year where many bookmakers also offer "specials" markets
- ✓ There is a very large number of players
- ✓ The players are matched up in pairs and threesomes which change from week to week
- ✓ There are usually at least 3 rounds of play
- ✓ There are additional "specials" markets offered by many bookmakers during the Majors
- ✓ It's possible to find hidden arbs by looking beyond the obvious in 2-ball match-ups

Golf trading specialist Fiona Hayes takes us through the techniques she uses.

"The arbs that crop up in the weekly 3-ball and 2-ball match-ups are fairly consistent. I put this down to the odds-compilers of a few bookies having quite strong opinions. To me it often seems as though they create some arbs deliberately just to get money in on the players they fancy to lose. But you can also create arbs in 2-ball using the different book-formats with different bookies. Some offer 2-ball match-ups with a Tie, usually at around 8/1, others just refund if there's a Tie."

This technique is similar to that described by Mark Dawson in the chapter on boxing, take a look at the example on the next page.

Example

BOOKMAKER	PLAYER 1	PLAYER 2	TIE
WILLIAM HILL	1.73	2.38	
VICTOR CHANDLER	1.50	3.00	8.00

Total percentage including Tie = 103.73%

	STAKES	PAYOUT	PROFIT
PLAYER 1	885.14	**964.06**	33.57
PLAYER 2	321.35	**964.06**	33.57
TIE	51.00	408.00+558.14=966.14	35.65
TOTAL STAKES	**930.49**		

"The matchplay tournaments are a little different and they throw up quite a few good 2-way arbitrage opportunities. They're easy to find and easy to place and because the tournaments are infrequent, the bookmakers struggle a little which leads to lots of arbs.

I do a lot of business during the Majors, with the normal 2 and 3-ball match-ups plus the various other markets put up by the bookies.

The "Make the Cut" markets can be excellent as the bookies have different ways of expressing the bets. Some do 2-way markets as in "will so-and-so player make the cut: yes or no" whilst others just do it as a 1-way bet as in "bet if you think so-and-so will make the cut".

Another variation is betting on how many rounds a player will go through – keep in mind that anyone who gets to the 3rd round has made the cut and you'll find lots of ways to create arbs.

The bookies also offer prices on highest and lowest scores for key players. This is well-worth looking into as most arbitrage-hunting software ignores these markets and sometimes the bookmakers overlap scores which can result in middles where you end up winning both bets. I had a corker 2 years ago with Phil Mickleson – I won nearly £1800 when my middle hit target during the US Open. Bets on finishing places are also worth checking out for the same reasons."

Motor Racing

Formula 1 has long been a rich source of arbs in a variety of markets. The ones I check are

> ➢ Driver match-ups (Qualification Race)
> ➢ Driver match-ups (Actual Race)
> ➢ Finish/Not finish (Qualification Race)
> ➢ Finish/Not finish (Actual Race)

The latter two are also sometimes known as Classification bets - being classified is, for the most part, the same as finishing. However, since classification requires the driver to have completed 90% of the laps, it is possible for a driver to be classified but not finish the race - if, for example, he crashes or his car stops sometime during the last 10% of the laps. This is obviously quite rare but you should be aware of the small risk if you decide to combine Finish/Not Finish bets with Classification bets.

NASCAR is an American event with 3 different series. The NASCAR NEXTEL Cup, Busch Grand National and Craftsman Truck Series drivers race every week towards the year-end championship. It's mainly the US-oriented bookmakers which price up these races and the main bets for arbs are driver match-ups for both the Qualification and Actual races.

Both Formula 1 and NASCAR match-ups have one thing in common that can make them a little awkward for manual searches; different bookmakers often pair up different drivers, unlike tennis for example, where the match-ups are always the same across the bookmakers.

Rugby

There are lots of interesting opportunities available in the sport of Rugby as Simon Ferguson explains:

"The thing is, rugby isn't supported quite as well as many other sports in terms of bookmaker time or the betting public. The fact that the bookies may not be as clued up on the sport obviously make it worth a closer look from an arbitrage trader's perspective.

Four straightforward arbitrage markets I look at are:

1. Match bets

2. Total points market

3. Handicap bets

4. Supremacy markets (Spread betting firms)

- ✓ *It pays to watch the bookmakers closely to see which ones are slow to react to news. I use www.rleague.com and www.rugbee.com for updates.*
- ✓ *I have found the total points markets can change quite dramatically, with different opinions based on projections of the weather. It's always worth checking for price updates if there is a change in weather.*
- ✓ *The handicap markets are similar to the match-bet markets except that they also occasionally throw up some nice middles.*

A Supremacy bet is basically a bet on how much one team will beat the other by. It takes the form of a spread-bet and is expressed as Favourite/Outsider/Price. The way you trade is by "buying" or "selling" the favourite.

For example:

Team (x) / Team (y) 20 – 23

In this example above you can see that the bookmaker believes that team (x) is the stronger side and that team (y) is predicted to lose with the points offered on the right.

So, you could take this bet by backing Team (x) to win by 23 points or more – to do this you would "buy" Team (x) at 23. If you bought team (x) "supremacy" at 23 for $10 and they followed by winning the match by 32 points, your win would be 32-23 x £10 = £90

It's in these points where the guaranteed profit opportunities are available. Using the example above, if you made a note of these points then visited another spread firm and they priced the match up a little differently like:

Team (x) / Team (y) 29 – 32.

Here you've got an opportunity to "buy" Team (x) supremacy at 23 and then immediately "sell" Team (x) with the second spread firm at 29.

Your profit is the difference between your buy and sell trades. In this case the win is six points. That's the difference between your 23 buy and your 29 sell. The result of the match has no bearing on your profit at this stage. Your only challenge is that these opportunities come and go fast. There are lots of them but they don't last long so you do need to have confidence and experience before taking on this market.

I find that spreads differ most in matches where there's a hot favourite leading to some spread firms being bold and offering their own opinions and between foreign clubs sides.

Fixed-Odds Middles

You have seen how the regular bookmakers run a "handicap" market for Rugby matches. It's in this market where it's possible to place a very good value bet that wins big when we win but only loses small when we lose.

For example, let's say you were quick to scour the prices of bookmakers' handicaps and saw that one bookmaker was offering the following price on the favourite team in a match:

Bookmaker 1

Team (x) – 10

Then you checked with another bookmaker and saw that they didn't give the favourite team such a big handicap with the following:

Bookmaker 2

Team (x) –2

You'd bet on Team (x) at Bookmaker 2 at – 2. You'd then place another equal bet on the other team at Bookmaker 1 at +10.

If Team (x) win by 3 to 9 points, both bets pay out.

One of the bets is always guaranteed to be a winner so if the results don't hit the middle the resultant loss is small.

Spread-bet vs. Fixed-Odds Middles

Another technique I like to use is combining spread supremacy bets with fixed-odds handicap bets to create middles & sometimes arbs. I'll explain with an example.

Supremacy bet: Team (x) / Team (y) 23-26

Fixed odds handicap bet: Team (x) -30 1.91

Team (y) +30 1.91

The trade: Buy Team (x) at 26 with a stop-loss at 22 and bet on Team (y) +30 at 1.91

The stop-loss gives your spread-trade a fixed value – the most you will lose is 4 points = £10 x 4 = £40. Now you can bet £44 on Team (y) +30 at 1.91

You've now got a 4-point middle:

If Team (x) wins by 27, 28, 29 or 30 points you will win the fixed-odds bet on Team (y) plus either £10, £20, £30 or £40 on the spread-bet on Team (x). i.e. Win between £40-£80

If Team (x) wins by 26 points or less, you will lose £40 on the spread-bet and win £40 on the fixed-odds bet on Team (y) i.e. Break-Even

If Team (x) wins by 31, 32, 33 or 34 points you will lose £44 on the fixed-odds bet and win £10, £20, £30 or £40 on the spread-bet i.e. lose £0-£30

If Team (x) wins by more than 34 points, you will win £10 per point above 34, with no limit.

Obviously these trades are not totally risk-free but as part of a balanced portfolio of arbs and middles, the certainly have their place and have made me some decent profit over the years."

Tennis

Tennis is, of course, the most popular sport for arbitrage traders. As I discovered quite early on in my trading career, the regularity of the weekly matches provides a routine of profits, punctuated by a major boost with the 4 grand slams. Some bookmakers issue prices on Sunday evenings (UK time) and the rest follow on Monday. It's harder these days to find tennis arbs manually because the services are so quick off the mark but, over the page, Mark Dawson has some tricks up his sleeve for finding arbs in tennis set-betting and handicaps. In general, I would strongly advise anyone who doesn't normally use a service to invest in one which uses software to find arbs, just for the grand slams. With a good service sending you arbs, it's fairly easy to make £1000 in the first week of one of these major tournaments.

I just want to say a little about tennis retirement rules as this is an area where I had my first taste of losses due to arbs going wrong. As you probably already know, tennis is one of the few sports in which bookmakers have varying rules of settlement in the event of match which is not completed due to a player retirement & it's important to be aware of potential ramifications. There are 3 main categories of settlement rules: Since Summer 2003, when a number of bookmakers who used to use the rule "All bets are action after the first ball is served" switched their rules, en masse, to "All bets are void if a match ends early due to retirement" it now appears to be much more likely that injuries will cause an arbitrageur a loss if the bets are between bookmakers with different rules. Many bookmakers, such as Bet & Win, Expekt, Olympic and Pinnacle are now extremely well informed about injuries. It's widely believed among arbers that Expekt actually set traps when they know about an injury. All this means is that you should not place mixed-rule tennis arbs indiscriminately - for example, if Expekt are out on a limb I would not place an arbitrage trade with them combined with a "No Action" bookmaker.

Set-betting is another source of tennis arbs and can be especially productive during the Grand Slams. These bets specify which player will win, and by what set-score. For example, in a 3-set match, the winner's score will be either 2-0 or 2-1. These bets provide an alternative way to hedge against a match bet on one of the players.

	PLAYER 1	PLAYER 2
BEST MATCH ODDS	1.30	4.00
BEST SET ODDS		
2-0	2.30	8.00
2-1	2.40	12.00

In this example, the best prices available on simple match-betting do not produce an arbitrage situation. However, by putting a bet on Hewitt to win the match (1.30) and combining that with bets on Gonzales to win 2-0 (8.00) and 2-1 (12.00) you have an arbitrage trade of just over 2%

PLAYER 1		PLAYER 2	
1.30	76.92%	8.00	12.50%
		12.00	8.33%
TOTAL PERCENTAGE		**97.76%**	

US Sports

Baseball (MLB)

With literally hundreds of matches playing out between April and October, MLB is the US sport which usually produces the most frequent arbs. Patrick Goodman explains the basics:

"Baseball is one of a few sports where we have bookmakers both sides of the Atlantic taking a keen interest. Here we have the classic opportunity to take advantage of differing opinions. American Sports Books have the professional Baseball odds compilers working for them whilst their Euro and UK counterparts don't. By mixing up US / UK and Euro prices, we should see regular bets occur.

US sportsbooks operate on considerably smaller profit margins than the UK and European Bookies. This is obviously very helpful as there is immediately less juice to beat when looking for arbs.

As a basic template, I'd suggest the following:

- ✓ *Compile a list of UK / US / Euro bookies that you wish to use for cross comparisons of the markets mentioned. Blue Square, Corals, Ladbrokes & Stan James in the UK can be good as they don't slavishly follow the US books' prices.*
- ✓ *UK traders need to start looking around mid afternoon, which is when most books start posting their prices for that evening's matches.*
- ✓ *If you find a difference in the "money line" with one particular bookmaker, double check the Run Line and Total Line as well as these might also be out of line.*
- ✓ *Throughout the Baseball season make comparisons between UK and US Bookmakers on future event bets. These bets will include:*

> ➢ *Outright winner of the World Series*
> ➢ *Outright winners of the respective leagues*
> ➢ *Outright winners of the six divisions within the two MLB leagues*

Making regular comparisons in these markets should pay well as UK Bookmakers don't update their prices within these markets as quickly as they do in the US. The divisional markets in particular are not as busy as other UK Sports so they are not highly prioritised. UK bookmakers have been known to be out of date quite frequently in the past. Arbs with percentages in the double-figures often come from these types of bets.

At the end of the season you can also trade between normal match-bets and the series bets. For example, if one team is ahead in the series and only needs to win 1 more match, then you can trade this match against the series"

However, baseball bets are not all the same, and it is important to be aware of the differences. The differences hang on the fact that many bookmakers price a team based upon which pitcher will be playing for them. If there is a change of pitcher, there may be a change in the bet. Some will void the bet ("no action") whilst others will consider it valid ("action")

Although this may seem to complicate matters, once you become familiar with the options, you will be able to enter a variety of arbitrage bets which have different degrees of risk. Pitcher changes during the early stages of the season are remote prospects. The players should all be pretty fit, and no-one should have lost form enough to be dropped to the Minor leagues yet. So only sudden illness or accident, or bereavement etc. should lead to a pitcher change.

Normally pitcher changes come through between 1 and 4 hours before the start. As the season takes its toll, changes get more frequent, especially where the original pitcher is pitching on less than 4 days' rest and, perhaps, pitched a lot of innings in his previous match.

Until you have more experience, stick to "both listed" with both legs of the trade on all arbs. That way you can never get a one-off loss.

Amir Bansil explains the various risk-profiles associated with the possible combinations:

THE RISK-FREE ARBITRAGE TYPE I

Some sites offer you a complete choice of pitcher options:

> - Action regardless of which pitchers start the game
> - Action only if one named pitcher starts; either on the team you are backing or their opponents
> - Action only if both named pitchers start

When dealing with bookies who offers these choices, your ideal bet structure will be:

> - Bet on team A with bookie A with the option of "no named pitchers" to start for team A or B
> - Bet on team B with bookie B with the option of "no named pitchers" to start for team A or B

Neither of these bets will be voided in the event of pitcher changes. Therefore, this is a standard arbitrage.

THE RISK-FREE ARBITRAGE TYPE II

Other sites do not offer the option of action regardless of starting pitcher. Your choices are to have action either on both named pitchers or the pitcher of the team you are backing.

When dealing with bookies who offers these choices, your ideal bet structure will be:

> - Bet on team A with bookie A with the option of "pitcher X" to start for team A.

> Bet on team B with bookie B with the option of "pitcher X" to start for team A.

This is a standard arbitrage and you will make the arb profit if X starts and break even if X does not.

THE RISK-FREE ARBITRAGE TYPE III

Some sites only offer action on both named pitchers. If bookie A in your arbitrage trade is one of these, place bets as follows:

> Bet on team A with bookie A with the option of "pitcher X" to start for team A, "pitcher Y" for team B
> Bet on team B with bookie B with the option of "pitcher X" to start for team A, "pitcher Y" for team B.

This is a standard arbitrage and you will make a profit if X and Y start and break even if either X or Y does not.

THE IMPERFECT ARBITRAGE

Some sites are "action only" which means that your bet will not void if there is a pitcher change. If bookie A is like this but bookie B is not, you will need to place bets as follows:

> Bet on team A with bookie A with the option of "no named pitchers" to start.
> Bet on team B with bookie B with the option of "pitcher Y" for team B.

You will make a standard profit if Y starts.

If Y does NOT start, then you will have one of the following scenarios:

> You get a windfall gain if A beats B since your stake on B is refunded.
> You suffer a loss if B beats A since your stake on B is refunded and the bet on A is lost.

ACTIVE ARBITRAGE TRADING

When there is a pitcher change there may well be a dramatic move in odds. This offers the potential for a really big arb. Suppose team B have changed their pitcher from Y to Z and their chances of winning are now reduced:

> Bet with Bookie A who hasn't yet moved his odds on team A for "action regardless" or "action if pitcher X starts"
> Bet with Bookie B on team B for "action regardless" or "action if pitcher X starts".

You are likely to secure arbs of over 10% doing this. But beware:

> You need to be watching what is going on and be really sure which team is changing pitcher and which bookie is behind
> You should keep your stakes within reason, since you will not know what the limits are at each bookie
> Make sure you get the bets on in the correct order, since in this case the bet on team A is much more attractive than the one on B."

Ice Hockey (NHL)

When the teams are not on strike, NHL provides a very large number of trades throughout the season, particularly between US and European bookmakers. But these bookmakers sometimes have different rules regarding their treatment of Overtime and this can affect the validity of the arbitrage trade.

On the plus side, these very differences can in rules can be exploited by "those in the know" to generate risk-free windfall profits as well as standard arbitrage profits.

An NHL match lasts for 60 minutes of Normal Time. If, after this period, one team has more points than the other, there is a winner and the match ends. However, if both teams have an equal score at this stage, it is considered a Tie in Normal Time and the teams play a 15-minute session of "sudden death" in which there can only be 1 point scored, and in which the winner of that point is deemed the winner of the match.

Moneyline Bets

These are normal non-handicapped bets where you bet on each team to win. With these bets, each bookmaker's rules on Overtime must be the same or there is a risk that you will lose both bets.

Example:

Bookmaker A does not include overtime

Bookmaker B includes overtime

Bet on Team 1 with Bookmaker A and bet on Team 2 with Bookmaker B

The following outcomes are possible at the end of Normal Time:

Team 1 wins: Bookmaker A pays out

Team 2 wins: Bookmaker B pays out

Tie: Bookmaker A refunds your stake but Bookmaker B's action is determined by the result after overtime

There are three possible outcomes at the end of overtime:

Tie (no point scored in overtime): Both bookmakers refund your stakes

Team 1 wins: Your stake was refunded by Bookmaker A because of the result in Normal Time but you lose your stake on Team 2

Team 2 wins: Your stake was refunded by Bookmaker A because of the result in Normal Time and you win your bet on Team 2

Totals (Under/Over)

With Ice Hockey Under/Overs you can combine bookies who have different treatments of overtime as long as the bookmaker you bet "Over" with includes overtime. In these cases, it is irrelevant whether or not the "Under" bookmaker includes overtime.

However, if the "Under" bookmaker does not include overtime, certain cases can result in a risk-free windfall profit in addition to the normal arbitrage.

Examples:

If the bets are Under/Over 4, the relevant possible outcomes are:

In normal time, score = 3 or score = 4 or score = 5

> ➢ If the score is 3, then the "Under 4" bet wins and no overtime is played i.e. Normal Arbitrage Profit
> ➢ If the score is 4, then either both bets will be refunded (if the match is not a Tie or if it is a Tie but there is no score in overtime) or the "Over 4" bet wins if there is point scored in overtime PLUS the "Under 4" bet is refunded (because the total

after Normal Time was exactly 4) i.e. Normal Arbitrage Profit + Windfall Gain

> If the score is 5 then no overtime will be played and the "Over 4" bet wins i.e. Normal Arbitrage Profit

If the bets are Under/Over 4.5, the relevant possible outcomes are:

In normal time, score = 3 or score = 4 or score = 5

> If the score is 3, then the "Under 4.5" bet wins and no overtime is played i.e. Normal Arbitrage Profit
> If the score is 4, then either the "Under 4.5" bet wins (if the match is not a Tie or if it is a Tie but there is no score in overtime) or the "Over 4.5" bet wins if there is point scored in overtime i.e. Normal Arbitrage Profit
> If the score is 5 then no overtime will be played and the "Over 4.5" bet wins i.e. Normal Arbitrage Profit

If the bets are Under/Over 5, the relevant possible outcomes are:

In normal time, score = 4 or score = 5 or score = 6

> If the score is 4 then either the "Under 5" bet wins (if the match is not a Tie or if it is a Tie but there is no score in overtime) or, if there is a point scored in overtime, the "Under 5" bet wins PLUS the "Over 5" bet is refunded (because the total after Overtime is exactly 5) i.e. Normal Arbitrage Profit + Windfall Gain
> If the score is 5, then no overtime will be played and both bets will be refunded i.e. Break-even Situation
> If the score is 6 then the "Over 5" bet wins i.e. Normal Arbitrage Profit

Handicap (Puckline) Bets

In cases where the spread (handicap) is +/-0.5 the situation is similar to that of Moneyline Bets AS LONG AS you ensure that the bookmaker who does not include overtime is the one who has assigned the positive handicap.

Example:

Bookmaker A does not include overtime

Bookmaker B includes overtime

Bet on Team 1 (+0.5) with Bookmaker A and bet on Team 2 (-0.5) with Bookmaker B

The following outcomes are possible at the end of Normal Time:

- ➢ Team 1 wins: Bookmaker A pays out i.e. Normal Arbitrage Profit
- ➢ Team 2 wins: Bookmaker B pays out i.e. Normal Arbitrage Profit
- ➢ Tie: Bookmaker A pays you as a winner but Bookmaker B's action is determined by the result after overtime i.e. Normal Arbitrage Profit + Potential Windfall

There are three possible outcomes at the end of overtime:

- ➢ Tie (no point scored in overtime): Bookmaker A pays you as a winner i.e. Normal Arbitrage Profit
- ➢ Team 1 wins: Bookmaker A pays you as a winner i.e. Normal Arbitrage Profit
- ➢ Team 2 wins: Bookmaker A pays you as a winner because of the Normal Time result and Bookmaker B pays you as a winner because of the Overtime result i.e. Normal Arbitrage Profit + Windfall Profit

However, if the handicaps are reversed, the following situations are possible:

Bet on Team 1 (-0.5) with Bookmaker A and bet on Team 2 (+0.5) with Bookmaker B

The following outcomes are possible at the end of Normal Time:

> - Team 1 wins: Bookmaker A pays out i.e. Normal Arbitrage Profit
> - Team 2 wins: Bookmaker B pays out i.e. Normal Arbitrage Profit
> - Tie: The bet with Bookmaker A is a loser but Bookmaker B's action is determined by the result after overtime i.e. Potential Risk To Capital

There are three possible outcomes at the end of overtime:

> - Tie (no point scored in overtime): Bookmaker B pays you as a winner i.e. Normal Arbitrage Profit
> - Team 1 wins: The bet with Bookmaker A is a loser because it is determined on the result after Normal Time i.e. Loss Of Capital
> - Team 2 wins: Bookmaker B pays you as a winner i.e. Normal Arbitrage Profit

In cases where the spread (handicap) is +/-1.5 the treatment of overtime doesn't matter and all arbs are risk-free with no potential windfall gain

Example:

Bookmaker A does not include overtime

Bookmaker B includes overtime

Bet on Team 1 (+1.5) with Bookmaker A and bet on Team 2 (-1.5) with Bookmaker B

The following outcomes are possible at the end of Normal Time:

- ➢ Team 1 wins: Bookmaker A pays out i.e. Normal Arbitrage Profit
- ➢ Team 2 wins: Bookmaker B pays out i.e. Normal Arbitrage Profit
- ➢ Tie: Bookmaker A pays out i.e. Normal Arbitrage Profit

There are three possible outcomes at the end of overtime:

- ➢ Tie (no point scored in overtime): Bookmaker A pays out i.e. Normal Arbitrage Profit
- ➢ Team 1 wins: Bookmaker A pays out i.e. Normal Arbitrage Profit
- ➢ Team 2 wins: Bookmaker A pays out i.e. Normal Arbitrage Profit

If the handicaps are reversed:

Bet on Team 1 (-1.5) with Bookmaker A and bet on Team 2 (+1.5) with Bookmaker B

The following outcomes are possible at the end of Normal Time:

- ➢ Team 1 wins by 2 points or more : Bookmaker A pays out i.e. Normal Arbitrage Profit
- ➢ Team 2 wins by any amount: Bookmaker B pays out i.e. Normal Arbitrage Profit
- ➢ Tie: Bookmaker B pays you as a winner i.e. Normal Arbitrage Profit

There are three possible outcomes at the end of overtime:

- ➢ Tie (no point scored in overtime): Bookmaker B pays you as a winner i.e. Normal Arbitrage Profit
- ➢ Team 1 wins: Bookmaker B pays you as a winner because the +1.5 handicap still places Team 2 ahead of team 1 i.e. Normal Arbitrage Profit
- ➢ Team 2 wins: Bookmaker B pays you as a winner i.e. Normal Arbitrage Profit

Multi-Currency Sports-Arbitrage Trades

Whilst it's possible for any UK-based trader to stick exclusively with Sterling accounts. However, the majority of offshore sportsbooks - those which specialise in US sports and payout "reload bonuses" and if you are prepared to open bookmaker accounts in US dollars, this increases the number of trading opportunities and can be very profitable if managed correctly.

Once you have made the decision to add a new currency to your portfolio, it pays to be organised. Funding foreign currency accounts on-the-fly with a credit card can be slow & expensive.

Accounting is another issue and different people have different ideas. I've outlined mine below as they are shared by the majority of professional traders I have spoken to. The way you account in the beginning will impact the way you have to account for each trade that you place using the new currency.

I decided at the outset to buy $10,000 with which to trade. With the exchange rate at 1.575, this cost me £6350. My plan was to place trades which may have had one side in Sterling with the other in Dollars, as well as trades in which both sides were in Dollars.

The stakes for the second type of trade are easy to calculate - it's just the same as for any arbitrage trade - all that changes is the currency symbol.

Example, for a total investment of £500

	ODDS	STAKE
PLAYER 1	2.00	£265
PLAYER 2	2.25	£235

If the 2 bookmakers held accounts in Dollars instead, the numbers are exactly the same for a total investment of $500:

	ODDS	STAKE
PLAYER 1	2.00	$265
PLAYER 2	2.25	$235

Some difficulties arise, however, when deciding how to treat trades where each side is in a different currency. How do you calculate the stakes? What rate do you use when calculating them? What happens if the rate changes by the time the bet settles and you end up with a notional loss? These questions perplexed me for a while and I tried a few different variations before settling on the method I use today.

I made the decision that I would consider myself a long-term dollar investor. This mindset instantly enabled me to disregard exchange rate fluctuations because they only matter when you actually want to change your money. So, I now only consider the rate at which I originally exchanged my dollars, and I use this rate in all of my stake calculations for arbs which combine Sterling and Dollars. I usually calculate both stakes as if everything was in Sterling and then I use the rate 1.575 to convert the Dollar leg of the trade. An example will make this clearer.

		ODDS
BOOKMAKER 1(£)	PLAYER 1	2.00
BOOKMAKER 2 ($)	PLAYER 2	2.25

First, I calculate the stakes in Pounds Sterling:

	ODDS	STAKE
PLAYER 1	2.00	£265
PLAYER 2	2.25	£235

Then I convert the Dollar side into Dollars using the rate 1.575:

£235 x 1.575 = $370 and this tells me exactly how I need to bet:

		ODDS	STAKE
BOOKMAKER 1(£)	PLAYER 1	2.00	£265
BOOKMAKER 2 ($)	PLAYER 2	2.25	$370

When the bets settle, I will receive either £530 (£265 x 2.00) or $832.50 ($370 x 2.25)

If I get £530 this means that in addition to the arbitrage profit, I have exchanged $370 of my Dollars into £235 at exactly the same rate that I originally bought the Dollars. If I get $832.50 then in addition to the arbitrage profit, I have exchanged £265 of my Sterling into Dollars at the same rate as all the rest of my Dollars. In both cases, the money stays in my trading pool and is continually used to trade as frequently as possible.

Now, whenever exchange rates are in favour of the Dollar i.e. better than or equal to 1.575 I may decide to change some back into Sterling. Whenever the exchange rate is worse than 1.575 I will just sit tight and continue to trade Dollar arbs. The point is that I am free to choose when I make the exchanges and I'll choose to do so when the rate suits me. The only way in which I can lose is if the Dollar never recovers and is always at a worse rate than 1.575 - this could happen but in that case, I've decided that I will simply use my Dollars to fund a family holiday for myself and my family!

Checklist

- ✓ Open an account with www.citibank.co.uk if possible. With this bank you can have free US Dollar and Euro accounts as well as the normal Sterling one. Any transfers you make between your accounts are made very close to the prevailing market rate so it is very cost-effective.
- ✓ Get a credit card with the Nationwide. This card doesn't attract the 2.5% fee that most other cards do when you transact in a foreign currency. The rate of exchange they give is pretty much the same as other cards i.e. not very good, but it's a good card to have for emergency situations.
- ✓ Open an account with www.neteller.com This is an "online wallet" which you can use to move your Dollars to and from bookmaker accounts, and to store the Dollars while they are not being used. Most bookmakers will let you withdraw to Neteller without any costs once per month and if you take advantage of this it is a very cost-effective solution. However, be careful of using Neteller to exchange your currency into another because they use shamelessly appalling rates. When you withdraw from your Neteller account ask for a Dollar cheque or have the money paid directly into your US Dollar bank account.

Betting Exchange Strategies

With Betfair currently leading the pack, there are a small number of liquid betting exchanges which provide a number of different types of trading opportunity.

Patrick Goodman explains the risk-free techniques he uses and some of the calculations behind them:

"There are 5 types of standard arbitrage trade that you can do with exchanges:

- ➤ Back at Bookmaker / Back at Exchange
- ➤ Back at Exchange 1 / Back at Exchange 2
- ➤ Back at Bookmaker / Lay at Exchange
- ➤ Back at Exchange 1 / Lay at Exchange 2
- ➤ Back at Exchange 1 / Lay at Exchange 1

1. Back at Bookmaker / Back at Exchange

This is the first and easiest type of arbitrage. Using an exchange in the place of the second bookmaker makes a small change to the way that stakes and profits are calculated because you have to take into account the commission that the exchange will take deduct from the winnings paid out on the bet placed at the exchange.

The most efficient way to calculate this is to build it into the price from the exchange at the very start. This lets you know immediately if there is a trade available with commission taken into account.

An example follows overleaf.

Example - first an arb with 2 bookmakers, investing £1000 in total:

	OUTCOME	ODDS	STAKE	TOTAL RECEIPTS
BOOKMAKER 1	PLAYER 1	2.00	£506	£1012
BOOKMAKER 2	PLAYER 2	2.05	£494	£1012

With no commissions to pay, it's all fairly straight-forward. Now let's replace Bookmaker 2 with an Exchange which is going to charge you a 5% commission of the profit if the bet with them wins

	OUTCOME	ODDS	STAKE	WIN	TOTAL RECEIPTS
BOOKMAKER 1	PLAYER 1	2.00	£506	£506	£1012
EXCHANGE	PLAYER 2	2.05	£494	£518	£1012-(5% x £518) = **£986**

In this example the arbitrage trade is destroyed by the exchange's commission. This is a regular occurrence so it can waste a lot of time if you have to go through this whole process each time just to see if an apparent arbitrage trade remains valid after the commission has been deducted.

So, instead of this, we can build the commission into the exchange's price. When both prices are then put into a calculator, it is immediately apparent whether or not the trade really exists at those prices.

The formula to build the exchange's commission into the price is simply

1 + [(Exchange Price - 1) x (100 - Exchange Commission)] /100

The Exchange Price is EU-style (i.e. 2.05 not 21/20).

To calculate what the real value of the price 2.05 we just use the formula. I'm going to continue with an Exchange Commission rate of 5% although obviously some exchanges are lower and the more active you are on exchanges the lower your rate becomes.

1 + [(2.05 - 1) x (100 - 5)] / 100 = 1 + (1.05 x 95) / 100 = 1 + 99.75 / 100 = 1 + 0.9975

= 1.9975

You can check this by seeing how much you would receive if you bet £494 at 1.9975:

£494 x 1.9975 = £986

The actual amount is £986.76 but I have been rounding off the pennies in all of the calculations above and this is the reason for the small discrepancy

Now, if you were to look at the same match but realise that the 2 prices you have got are really 2.00 at the bookies and 1.9975 at the exchange, you won't bother with it because you can see straight away that it is not an arbitrage trade.

2. Back at Exchange 1 / Back at Exchange 2

The next type of arbitrage trade is when you replace both bookies with different exchanges:

	OUTCOME	ODDS	STAKE	TOTAL RECEIPTS
EXCHANGE 1	PLAYER 1	2.10	£506	£1012 – COMMISSION
EXCHANGE 2	PLAYER 2	2.25	£494	£1012 – COMMISSION

Although there are 2 commissions involved only one is going to be payable because only one of the bets will win. The way to handle this is to calculate the maximum commission payable and see how this affects the arb - if the arb remains valid after this deduction then you can trade it.

The side of the arb which involves the highest commissions depends on the commission rate and the odds. In practical terms, since exchange commissions are usually very similar this means that the bet with the highest odds will usually generate the highest commission (if your commission rates vary then you should work out each separately)

Example - both exchanges charge 5%

	OUTCOME	ODDS	STAKE	WIN	COMMISSION
EXCHANGE 1	PLAYER 1	2.10	£506	£1012	(£1012 – £506) x 0.05 = **£25.30**
EXCHANGE 2	PLAYER 2	2.25	£494	£1012	(£1012 – £494) x 0.05 = **£25.30**

3. Back at Bookmaker / Lay at Exchange

With this type of trade, you're using the LAY price at an exchange so the calculations change slightly.

The idea is to find a high price at a bookmaker to back the selection and then Lay the same selection at an exchange, at a better price, and pocket the difference whether the selection wins or loses. Of course, if the selection loses then you will pay a commission at the exchange.

This type of trading can be very profitable and it even works with offline bookmakers so if you live in the UK and can get to the bookmaker shops, it's easy to generate £400-£500 each month from this technique alone. The best sport to trade this way is soccer

Offline, use Corals, Ladbrokes & William Hill &keep your bets below £500 to avoid attention when you win at the bookmaker. Always ask the counter clerk to phone their head office to confirm that the price on the coupon is what you will get on your bet - this is important as they sometimes update their prices on their screens but obviously not on the coupons which are printed out.

If you start taking Coral coupon odds and laying them on the exchanges on a weekly basis then you will soon realise that there are plenty of other coral odds that are not so obvious and which can also be laid on exchanges. These non-soccer bets win at the bookmaker less often which balances the wins you will often take from them on the soccer bets. With practice you will begin to see when a price is out of line when the bookmaker puts his prices up before the exchanges do. Once you can do this then your profits can easily double as you will be backing early prices - then laying them at a profit (or at worst, break-even) on the exchanges later. If you are waiting to back a coupon price when it becomes profitable to do so on an exchange this is a fine strategy but you will be missing out a lot of profits.

For my calculations, I simply convert the Lay price into its equivalent backing price and then use this number to work out my stakes. The formula is:

Backing Price = 1 + 1 / (Lay Price - 1)

When you do this you give yourself a price to back the selection to lose. The example below should make this clearer.

Example

Let's say that I backed a football team at a bookie to win its match on Saturday at the price 1.61 and I now want to Lay this team at an exchange where the Lay price is currently 1.50

I already know that there is some profit in the trade because the Lay price is lower than the price I backed at (you always want to Back as high as possible and Lay as low as possible - in the early days I remembered this rule by saying BACK UP / LAY DOWN)

To calculate my stakes, I just convert the Lay price into an equivalent backing price and use my normal arbitrage spreadsheet:

Backing Price = 1 + 1 / (Lay Price - 1)

Backing Price = 1 + 1 / (1.50 - 1) = 1 + 1/(0.50) = 1 + 2 = 3.00 in EU-style odds

So, now I have the following situation, investing £1000:

	OUTCOME	ODDS	STAKE	TOTAL RECEIPTS
BOOKMAKER	TEAM TO WIN	1.61	£651	£1048
EXCHANGE	TEAM TO LOSE	3.00	£349	£1048 - COMMISSION

Now I just build in the exchange's commission into the price (as explained on the previous page):

The formula to build the exchange's commission into the price is simply

1 + [(Exchange Price - 1) x (100 - Exchange Commission)] /100

1 + [(3.00 - 1) x (100 - 5)] / 100 = 1 + (2 x 95) / 100 = **2.90**

So my stakes and returns will be:

	OUTCOME	ODDS	STAKE	TOTAL RECEIPTS
BOOKMAKER	TEAM TO WIN	1.61	£651	£1035
EXCHANGE	TEAM TO LOSE	3.00	£349	£1035

4. Back at Exchange 1 / Lay at Exchange 2

This technique is similar to that above - the only difference is that you will replace the bookmaker with another exchange. Although there are 2 commissions involved only one is going to be payable because only one of the bets will win. The way to handle this is to calculate the maximum commission payable and see how this affects the trade - if it remains valid after this deduction then you can trade it.

	OUTCOME	ODDS
EXCHANGE 1	BACK PLAYER 1	2.10
EXCHANGE 2	LAY PLAYER 1	1.95

Again, I convert the Lay price into an equivalent Back price using the formula:

Backing Price = 1 + 1 / (Lay Price - 1) = 1 + 1 / (1.95 - 1) = 2.05

This is the price that you are **effectively backing Player 2** (because you are betting on Player 1 to lose)

	OUTCOME	ODDS	STAKE	TOTAL RECEIPTS
EXCHANGE 1	BACK PLAYER 1	2.10	£494	£1037 – COMMISSION
EXCHANGE 2	BACK PLAYER 2	2.05	£506	£1037 – COMMISSION

Then I consider which commission will be the larger of the 2 [In practical terms, since exchange commissions are usually very similar this means that the bet with the highest odds will usually generate the highest commission (if your commission rates vary then you should work out each separately)] and build this into the price:

1 + [(Exchange Price - 1) x (100 - Exchange Commission)] /100

1 + [(2.10 - 1) x (100 - 5)] / 100 = 1 + (1.10 x 95) / 100 = **2.045**

The trade now looks like this:

	OUTCOME	ODDS	STAKE	TOTAL RECEIPTS	PROFIT
EXCHANGE 1	BACK PLAYER 1	2.045	£501	£1024	£24
EXCHANGE 2	BACK PLAYER 2	2.05	£499	£1024	£24

5. Back at Exchange 1 / Lay at Exchange 1

This is an extremely powerful technique which requires a little more market knowledge but which works very well because it reduces the amount of commission you pay to the exchange on your trades.

	OUTCOME	ODDS
EXCHANGE 1	BACK PLAYER 1	2.10
EXCHANGE 2	LAY PLAYER 1	1.95

Again, I convert the Lay price into an equivalent Back price using the formula:

Backing Price = 1 + 1 / (Lay Price - 1) = 1 + 1 / (1.95 - 1) = 2.05

	OUTCOME	ODDS	STAKE	TOTAL RECEIPTS
EXCHANGE 1	BACK PLAYER 1	2.10	£494	£1037 – COMMISSION
EXCHANGE 2	BACK PLAYER 2	2.05	£506	£1037 – COMMISSION

The difference here is that **you are only going to pay a commission on your profit, not on your total winnings**. This is a very important concept.

Previously, we had to calculate the commission on the winning on the bet.

For example, if we bet £494 at 2.10 the winnings are (£494 x 2.10) - £494 = £543

The commission would be 5% of £543 = £27.15

However, in this case, although we have won £543 on the bet, we have **also lost £506 in the same market with the same exchange.** The exchange looks at the **net win** and this equates to £37

So, the commission payable would be 5% of £37 = £1.85

You can see that this trade is exactly the same as the one on the previous page except that we use the same exchange. Look at the staggering difference it makes on the profitability of the trade.

Leveraging Existing Arbitrage Trades

This technique is an excellent way to create extra value from an existing arbitrage trade, reduce commissions and gain free reuse of your betting bank whilst waiting for bets to settle.

Whenever you place a trade which involves backing an outcome at a bookmaker and laying the same outcome at an exchange, the opportunity to get another arbitrage trade exists - by backing the outcome on the exchange - because the trade would be commission free.

For example if you backed Leeds against Millwall for £500 at 2.20 and lay £545 the bet off on the exchanges at 2.06. You now have a liability on the exchange of £577.70 on Leeds. That is, if Leeds win you will lose £577.70 on the exchange (and win £600 from the bookmaker).

	OUTCOME	ODDS	STAKE	IF LEEDS WIN	IF LEEDS LOSE
BOOKMAKER	BACK LEEDS	2.20	£500	+£600	-£500
EXCHANGE	LAY LEEDS	2.06	£545	- £577.50	+£545 (- COMMISSION)

Later on during the week, the prices have changed and Leeds can be backed at 2.10 with the same exchange and the +1 handicap on Millwall can be backed at 1.95

Assuming that you have to pay a commission of 5% to the exchange, this new trade is not worth doing. However, you already have a liability of £577.70 on Leeds at the exchange so you can now back Leeds up to £577.70 without paying any commission

This allows you to take the second trade by backing Leeds at 2.10 and backing Millwall (+1) at 1.95 for a 1% profit - and you will no longer have to pay the commission on the first trade.

There are many opportunities each week to benefit from such situations. In fact, you can even create them for yourself by placing break-even trades, backing at the bookmaker and laying at the exchange in anticipation of price-movements later in the week. If the price movement occurs you can then place the second trade and make money. If it does not then you simply leave the trade alone and break-even.

When you consider the hundreds of football matches which take place each week, you start to see just how profitable this type of trading can be.

Trading With Accumulators

An accumulator bet is a type of bet which depends on multiple outcomes being guessed correctly. For example, the bet may be "Team 1 to win its match against Team 2 AND Team 3 to win its mach against Team 4". This bet only wins if both of the outcomes are correct.

Traditionally thought of as useless for arbitrage trading, accumulator bets can actually be used to create regular trading profits.

This technique works best with European soccer but you can use it with pretty much any sport where the 2 (if it's a double) or 3 (if it's a treble) matches have a little bit of time between each other. The idea is to place a bet on the accumulator first and then hedge each bet before the relevant match begins. You are guaranteed a profit regardless but this profit increases the longer the accumulator runs. You need to get the bets on at the bookmaker very early in the week as the prices on the favourites tend to go down as the matches get closer.

Here's an example.

Consider a £100 treble which I bet a few weeks ago:

Kiev 1.57
CSKA 2.10
Werder2.20

Stage 1

Lay Kiev on an exchange. I did this at Betfair at 1.50, laying £102

The possible scenarios were:

Kiev Lose: My £100 at the bookmaker is lost and I gain £102 on the exchange. The accumulator stops here with a £2 profit on the trade.

Kiev Win: I lose £53 at the exchange whilst my £100 bet at the bookmaker wins and becomes £157. This £157 is automatically placed on CSKA at 2.10 and the accumulator goes to stage 2

Stage 2

Lay CSKA on an exchange. I did this at 1.91, laying £173

The possible scenarios were:

CSKA Lose: My £157 at the bookmaker is lost and I gain £173 on the exchange. The accumulator stops here with a £16 profit on the trade.

CSKA Win: I lose £157.43 at the exchange whilst my £157 bet at the bookmaker wins and becomes £329.70. This £329.70 is automatically placed on Werder at 2.20 and the accumulator goes to stage 3

Stage 3

Lay Werder on an exchange. I did this at 2.00, laying £362.50

The possible scenarios were:

Werder Lose: My £329.70 at the bookmaker is lost and I gain £362.50 on the exchange. The accumulator stops here with a £32.80 profit on the trade.

Werder Win: I lose £362.50 at the exchange whilst my £329.70 bet at the bookmaker wins and I receive the stake (£329.70) plus a win of 395.64 so the total profit of the trade is £33.14

There are literally hundreds of these types of opportunities every month and the more bets you include in the multiple the more you potentially stand to win. However, before you go above trebles, think about how much capital you have left over to cover your bets at the exchanges - you can see that by Stage 3, I needed £362.50 to cover my bets even though it all started with a £100 accumulator.

This technique provides an additional benefit: betting accumulators with your bookmakers will disguise your activity as an arbitrage trader as this type of bet is generally thought of as being the tool of the traditional 'mug punter'

You can also trade some doubles and trebles using the Betfair 'Accumulators' section for most of the major leagues and coupons.

However, there are some potential problems that you should be aware of:

1) Watch the 'kick off' time of the accumulators. They all get suspended together as a group usually when the first game kicks off.

2) The liquidity is often low, probably for the reasons mentioned below.

3) If you lay a multiple and one leg is postponed then the whole accumulator is void on Betfair. However, your bet with the bookies will still run minus one selection.

4) If you lay a double with one game on Tuesday and one on Wednesday and the Tuesday game loses, then Betfair will wait until after the Wednesday game is played before paying you out. If the Wednesday game is cancelled the (losing) accumulator is void at Betfair but your bet with the bookmaker loses.

For these reasons I much prefer to stick to the method on the previous page.

Bonus-Hunting

Using bookmaker bonuses to their full potential is a must for any trader. It is probably the single easiest way to make money on the internet!

The first type of bonus you will receive will be a sign-up bonus when you make your first deposit. Not all bookmakers offer this but most do. Some may offer "free bets" which are effectively the same thing. Others may restrict the free bets to multiples-only but if you have read the previous chapter on Accumulators Strategy then you will know that even these are worth considerable profits.

The other, more interesting, bonuses are offered at various times of the year by many bookmakers. These are the "reload" or "re-deposit" bonuses and they are usually offered every week in February & March, in the lead up to and during the basketball period known as March Madness, and in September at the start of the NFL season. However, some bookmakers do make these promotional offers at other times of the year as it is a good way for them to generate business. Make sure that you pay attention to the emails you receive from the bookmakers - they may seem like junk but you do not want to miss an invitation to receive a reload bonus.

Since some of these bonuses are with overseas bookmakers who often denominate accounts in US dollars, you may wish to review the chapter on trading with multiple currencies before getting too heavily involved with these bonuses.

The bookmakers will give you a bonus when you make a new deposit but they will have conditions which usually require that you bet the deposit and the bonus a few times over before you can withdraw. Obviously, they expect most gamblers to lose the money. However, traders like you and I are able to take the money and run using the techniques described below.

The basic premise is to bet your deposit and bonus on an event and then hedge it elsewhere - if the original bet loses then the hedge will win and you can withdraw the entire amount from the bookmaker or exchange with which you hedged. If the original bet wins then you have moved towards fulfilling the withdrawal conditions set by the bookmaker and you simply repeat the process. The variations below can be used in any combination depending on your goals and circumstances - they just vary in terms of the amount of time and effort required and the amount of profit they generate.

The quick & easy way to generate over £1000, risk-free is to take up the free bets & bonuses from bookmakers and simply lay them off at an exchange. Here is an example:

In this example, we take advantage of VCBet's offer of a £50 free bet for new customers. According to the rules at VCBet regarding this bonus, our bet must be placed at odds equal to or higher than 1/1 (aka evens or 2.00). We first have to place a bet with VCBet using our own funds in order to qualify for the free bet. We'll lay the bet off at Betfair for a very small loss.

First bet (placed in order to qualify for the free bet)				
Bookmaker	Bet Type	Outcome	Stake	Price
VCBet	Back	Newcastle	£50	2.90
Betfair	Lay	Newcastle	£50.52	2.92

With the bets above:

- If Newcastle wins, we will receive £95 from VCBet and lose £97 at Betfair i.e. a loss of £2
- If Newcastle does not win (i.e. draw/lose), we lose £50 at VCBet and win (after commission) £48 at Betfair i.e. a loss of £2

Having lost £2, however, we now have a free £50 bet to use.

Using the free bet				
Bookmaker	Bet Type	Outcome	Stake	Price
VCBet	Back	Derby	£50	4.35
Betfair	Lay	Derby	£36.02	4.70

With the bets on the previous page:

- If Derby wins, we will receive £167.50 from VCBet and lose £133.28 at Betfair i.e. a profit of £34.22
- If Derby does not win (i.e. draw/lose), we lose £50 at VCBet and win (after commission) £34.22 at Betfair i.e. a profit of £34.22

Taking into account the £2 lost in the first phase of this operation, the net profit from this free bet is £32.22

£32.22 may not sound like much but you can easily repeat this same process 40 times over the course of a week to make well over £1000 completely risk-free. With the follow-up bonuses offered by most of the bookmakers, your total profit could be as much as £5000 - just for doing the preparation work you need to anyway if you want to become a sports-arbitrage trader!

Visit the following link right now for an up-to-date list of bookmakers whose bonuses you can use to earn over £1000 in the next few days:

http://www.sportsarbitrageworld.com/freebets.htm

The following techniques take a little more time & effort but they can be more profitable. I'm using recent real-life examples of bookmakers and the bonuses they offered:

INTERTOPS: 20% RELOAD, BODOG 10% RELOAD, BETINTERNET 10% RELOAD

✓ **Method 1: Least effort, lowest profit - Simple Hedging**

BOOKMAKER	DEPOSIT	BONUS	TOTAL
INTERTOPS	$500	$100	$600
PINNACLESPORTS	$600	0	$600

Intertops pays a 20% bonus on the $500 deposit while Pinnacle offers no bonus. The best games to use are US sports because the bookmakers generally have very low margins on them. Just find a game that takes place later today and that both bookmakers have prices for:

BOOKMAKER	TEAM 1	TEAM 2	STAKE T1	STAKE T2	RESULTS T1 WINS	T2 WINS
INTERTOPS	1.91	1.91	$600	0	$1145.45	0
PINNACLESPORTS	1.91	1.91	0	$600	0	$1145.45

You stake a total of $1200 (but this only cost you $1100 because $100 was a free bonus) and your guaranteed return is $1145.45. In other words, you have made a guaranteed profit of $45.45

The ideal result would be that Team 2 wins because then the winnings will all come from Pinnacle and you can withdraw whenever you want to. However, if Team 1 wins then the bet counts towards Intertops conditions of withdrawal and you just have to repeat the process.

✓ **Method 2: A little more effort, slightly better profits - Finding a 100% book**

BOOKMAKER	DEPOSIT	BONUS	TOTAL
BODOG	$1000	$100	$1100
PINNACLESPORTS	$1210	0	$1210

With this method you need to find a game where the bookmakers have slightly different opinions - not so great as to create an arb but enough to create a break-even situation between the bets.

BOOKMAKER	TEAM 1	TEAM 2	STAKE T1	STAKE T2	RESULTS T1 WINS	T2 WINS
BODOG	2.10	1.80	$1100	0	$2310	0
PINNACLESPORTS	1.91	1.91	0	$1210	0	$2310

You stake a total of $2310 (but this only cost you $2210 because $100 was a free bonus) and your guaranteed return is $2310. In other words, you have made a guaranteed profit of $100. The ideal result would be that Team 2 wins because then the winnings will all come from Pinnacle and you can withdraw whenever you want to. However, if Team 1 wins then the bet counts towards Bodog's conditions of withdrawal and you just have to repeat the process.

✓ Method 3: Using double bonuses

BOOKMAKER	DEPOSIT	BONUS	TOTAL
BODOG	$1000	$100	$1100
BETINTERNET	$1110	$100	$1210

In this example, we find a game where the bookmakers have slightly different opinions - not so great as to create an arbitrage trade but enough to create a break-even situation between the bets. However, you could just use Method 1's simple hedging for less profit if you don't have the time to look for a 100% book.

					RESULTS	
BOOKMAKER	TEAM 1	TEAM 2	STAKE T1	STAKE T2	T1 WINS	T2 WINS
BODOG	2.10	1.80	$1100	0	$2310	0
BETINTERNET	1.91	1.91	0	$1210	0	$2310

You stake a total of $2310 (but this only cost you $2110 because you got $200 in free bonuses) and your guaranteed return is $2310. In other words, you have made a guaranteed profit of $200.

Whatever the result is, we free the deposit and bonus from one bookie and move towards fulfilling the withdrawal requirements of the other. You would then just repeat the process.

✓ Method 4: Using arbitrage

BOOKMAKER	DEPOSIT	BONUS	TOTAL
INTERTOPS	$500	$100	$600
BETINTERNET	$630	$63	$693

This is usually the most time-consuming method but it's by far the most profitable because you only place your bets when there is an arbitrage trade available. It's important to be organised so you know exactly where your bonuses are sitting and it really helps if you are using ArbAlarm so you don't have to spend too much time searching. ArbAlarm will also send you break-even trades (100% books), if you set your filters accordingly, and these are obviously very useful for the techniques described here.

					RESULTS	
BOOKMAKER	TEAM 1	TEAM 2	STAKE T1	STAKE T2	T1 WINS	T2 WINS
INTERTOPS	2.20	1.73	$600	0	$1320	0
BETINTERNET	1.91	1.91	0	$693	0	$1323

You stake a total of $1293 (but this only cost you $1130 because you got $163 in free bonuses) and your guaranteed return is $1320 if Team 1

wins and $1323 if team 2 wins (the differences are due to rounding). In other words, you have made a guaranteed profit of either $190 or $193.

Whatever the result is, we free the deposit and bonus from one bookie and move towards fulfilling the withdrawal requirements of the other. You would then just repeat the process.

You can use a combination of all of these methods to free your bonuses. Whenever arbitrage trades are available obviously you should take them but it's not necessary to stick to the same method after that. For example, you might use Method 4 first and then go to Method 2 until you are able to withdraw my money.

Middles & Sides

Middles and Sides are a type of low-risk or sometimes risk-free trade which can result in a windfall payment. A successful Middle results in both sides of the trade winning and a successful Side will result in one bet winning and the other having its stake returned.

Why bother with middles?

A very risk averse, pure arbitrage bettor will not be interested in middles since some risk is involved in over 90% of them. However, anyone else involved in betting should be interested for the following reasons:

- ✓ **They produce high returns**. My average arb bet yields around 2.7%. The average expected return on my middles so far is 7% with actual returns of 5%.
- ✓ **They are easier to find than arbitrage trades**. Most weekends you can find 5 or 6 decent NFL middles for one hour's work. If

there are more than 5 NBA games in an evening you can usually find at least 1 Middle.

- ✓ **They are often fond with arbs**. When looking for middles I usually find 1 or 2 decent arbs at the same time, in moneylines, handicaps or totals.
- ✓ **It seems that bookmakers may be more relaxed about being middled than being arbed**. The fact is that in most sports the spread comes into play less than 20% of the time. The other 80% either the dog wins outright, or the favourite wins by more than the spread so it may not be obvious to the bookmaker that your bet was a middle, This may help your standing with him if you are also a prolific arbitrage trader..

Middles are Sides generally occur in2 types of bet - handicap match-bets and Totals when 2 or more bookmakers disagree with either the handicap or the total to the extent that the ranges overlap.

For example, consider 2 bookmakers pricing up the handicaps in a game between 2 teams:

	TEAM 1 PRICE: HANDICAP	TEAM 2 PRICE: HANDICAP
BOOKMAKER 1	+8 : 1.91	-8 : 1.91
BOOKMAKER 2	+6 : 1.91	-6 : 1.91

The handicaps overlap as Bookmaker 1 shows +8 whilst Bookmaker 2 shows -6. If you were to bet a total of £200 on this middle:

	BET	RETURN
BOOKMAKER 1 / TEAM 1	£100 @ 1.91	£190.91
BOOKMAKER 2 / TEAM 2	£100 @ 1.91	£190.91

The following results are possible:

OUTCOME	BET RESULT	PROFIT/LOSS
TEAM 1 LOSES BY MORE THAN 8 POINTS	BET ON TEAM 2 WINS	£190.91 - £200 = **-£9.09**
TEAM 1 LOSES BY 6 POINTS	BET ON TEAM 1 WINS + BET ON TEAM 2 VOID = **SUCCESSFUL SIDE**	(£190.91 + £100) - £200 = **+£90.91**
TEAM 1 LOSES BY 8 POINTS	BET ON TEAM 2 WINS + BET ON TEAM 1 VOID = **SUCCESSFUL SIDE**	(£190.91 + £100) - £200 = **+£90.91**
TEAM 1 LOSES BY 7 POINTS	BET ON TEAM 1 WINS + BET ON TEAM 2 WINS = **SUCCESSFUL MIDDLE**	(£190.91 + £190.91) - £200 = **+£181.82**
TEAM 1 WINS	BET ON TEAM 1 WINS	£190.91 - £200 = - **£9.09**

So you can see that there is 1 scenario which gives us a successful middle, 2 which give us successful sides and 2 which result in a small loss.

Overleaf is an example using a Total Points (Under/Over) market:

BOOKMAKER 1	UNDER 35 : PRICE 1.91	OVER 35 : PRICE 1.91
BOOKMAKER 2	UNDER 45 : PRICE 1.91	OVER 45 : PRICE 1.91

The Totals overlap as Bookmaker 1 shows Over 35 whilst Bookmaker 2 shows Under 45. If you were to bet a total of £200 on this middle:

	BET	RETURN
BOOKMAKER 1 / OVER 35	£100 @ 1.91	£190.91
BOOKMAKER 2 / UNDER 45	£100 @ 1.91	£190.91

The following results are possible:

OUTCOME	BET RESULT	PROFIT/LOSS
TOTAL: UNDER 35	BET ON UNDER 45 WINS	£190.91 - £200 = **-£9.09**
TOTAL: EXACTLY 35	BET ON UNDER 45 WINS + BET ON OVER 35 VOID = **SUCCESSFUL SIDE**	(£190.91 + £100) - £200 = **+£90.91**
TOTAL: EXACTLY 45	BET OVER 35 WINS + BET ON UNDER 45 VOID = **SUCCESSFUL SIDE**	(£190.91 + £100) - £200 = **+£90.91**
TOTAL: 36, 37, 38, 39, 40, 41, 42, 43 OR 44	BET ON OVER 35 WINS + BET ON UNDER 45 WINS = **SUCCESSFUL MIDDLE**	(£190.91 + £190.91) - £200 = **+£181.82**
TOTAL: OVER 45	BET ON OVER 35 WINS	£190.91 - £200 = **-£9.09**

Here there is a range of scores which will give us a successful middle, 2 which give us successful sides and 2 which result in a small loss.

The larger the overlap in prices, the better the middle

Reverse Middles

Key Numbers

Key numbers – also sometimes known as trap numbers – are an important factor in evaluating the true worth of a middle. To explore these in more detail, let's look at American Football results in the period 1982 to 2001.

For most spreads (handicaps), the outcome of the match finished on the spread 5-6% of the time. However, there were 3 numbers which this rule of thumb didn't apply to:

- Just over 10% of matches priced at +7 finished at +7.
- Just over 10% of matches priced at +3 finished at +3.
- Well under 1% of matches finished on 0 (a tie).

The reasons arise in the way the game is scored. Ties virtually never arise because there is usually a score in overtime – always check your bookmakers both count overtime when placing NFL middles. The scoring in NFL is 3 points for field goals, 5 for a touchdown and 2 for a conversion – conversions are rarely missed.

So the scoring mostly goes up by 3 or 7 each time. These are the key numbers for NFL. This means that, if both bets are priced at –110, all of the following middles have expected values over 5%:

- A middle of +4 and –2.5, or +3.5 and –2 (8%)
- A middle of +4.5 and –3, or +3 and –1.5 (6%)
- A middle of +8 and –6.5, or +7.5 and –6 (8%)
- A middle of +8.5 and –7, or +7 and –5.5 (6%)
- A 3 point middle where 0 is in the middle since 0 more or less never happens (7%)
- A 2 point middle for all other spreads under 15 (7%)

So a 1.5 middle with 3 or 7 in the middle is a better bet than a 3-point middle with 0 in the middle.

Buying Points

Frequently when you are middling you come across the following decision to make. Let's say a team is +6 and −110 with one bookmaker. Team 2 has the following bets available and you are unsure which way to middle the game:

Bookie A is offering −4.5 at −110, Bookie B is −4 at -120.

The prospect for a middle is better with B but you have to pay worse odds for the privilege. in general it is usually worth buying an extra 0.5 point if this brings a key number into play, and usually you need a full extra point for non-key numbers

Managing your Middles betting bank

I recommend that you focus on the potential losses and aim to limit them. Let the potential gains look after themselves. I use the following process:

• I have a middling "bank" of notional capital.
• I then allocate a fixed percentage of this – usually 2% - as the maximum loss I will accept on an individual middle. Bear in mind I may have up to 10 of these running at one time, so this means having 20% of the bank at risk at once.
• I log in to the bookmakers' sites I want to bet on.
• I go through all the menus until I reach the final "Place bet" screen on both sites, with the stakes I intend to place keyed in.
• I now bet on the leg I believe to be the more attractive price, given the prices generally available.
• I now bet on the second leg.
• I record both bets in my "bank" spreadsheet and the expected loss if the bet doesn't middle.

This method aims to preserve as much of my capital as possible during bad runs, ready for the joyous time when I hit a hot streak. In the hot streak, my "bank" builds up and my stakes rapidly increase.

These prices are not as volatile as prices on which a straight arbitrage is available. But there can often be some big line moves, especially when team changes are made. So it pays to bet the more attractive price first since this line is more likely to move against you.

Best sports to Middle

In theory any sport in which handicaps exist offers potential middles. In practice sports like soccer where scoring is low are unlikely to offer middles, you need high scoring matches:

• American football and basketball are both very good.
• Rugby union and rugby league are also good, with similar key numbers to NFL.
• Cricket Total Runs are often excellent for middling opportunities
• The games handicaps in tennis can be good but not many bookies offer this.
• When snooker handicaps are offered, middles can occur.
• Special bets offered on soccer championships can be very good - for example during the World Cup many bookmakers will offer "Total number of goals scored in the entire tournament"

One point to be wary of is that many UK bookies offer the following set-up for rugby:

Wasps+7 10/11
Tie+7 15/1
Tigers-7 10/11

This means that if the Tigers win by 7, and you have bet this option, this bet loses. (If only 2 options are offered, this means it "pushes" and you get your stake back.) In these cases, I evaluate the Tigers as –7.5 instead of –7 since an 8 point win by the Tigers is the lowest margin at which I don't lose this bet.

There are two main factors in setting odds for handicaps which increase the chances of finding middles – differences of opinion and line volatility.

Arbitrage traders will be familiar with both of these, but I will give some specific examples with regard to middles. In rugby, especially internationals, when bookies first set lines there is often a variety of views on what the true handicaps should be. This variety is likely to narrow as time passes, so as with arbitrage betting it is wise to snap up good middles before the lines move.

In US sports most internet books initially just set their lines to be the same as the "Vegas" line, then adjust them as time passes according to supply and demand on their books. Low margin bookmakers like Pinnacle will usually see high initial demand for favourites, then high demand for underdogs on match day. This is because professionals tend to bet the favourites early and the under dogs late . Bookmakers with a high proportion of mug punter customers such as Sports Interaction will see high demand for the favourites on match day – so you can often find a good middle between a square book and a sharp book.

US sports are not a major market for most European books. They tend to put their lines down early and follow the Vegas handicaps. Some do not then monitor these markets closely, probably feeling that their –110 and –120 lines are pretty well arb-proof so there is little risk of an unbalanced book. Meanwhile, the US books will move their spreads aggressively in response to team and pitch news, as well as steam chasing and similar betting action. So you can often middle between a US book which has reacted to recent developments and a European book which may not even monitor these. Most Sunday evenings you will be able to find the following sort of opportunity:

Steelers+3 +110
Bears-4 +110

If the Bears were handicapped at –3, this would be a risk-free bet. You could bet £110 on each and win £10 whether the Bears or Steelers win.

But the Bears are at –4, which is why this bet is called a reverse middle (or Polish middle). If the Bears win by 4 or 3, you lose £110 since the other bet will "push". Is it worthwhile?

In this example it is more or less break-even, since there is a 10% chance of a –3 result here. If this reverse middle was +8 and –9 (or any other pairing which does not include a key number) then this bet will have an expected value of 1.7%. (It is a "pseudo arb" – arbitrage odds are available, and although the situation is not risk-free it is still worth doing.) Normally these sorts of odds are only available around a key number, those with decent positive expectations do not last long. I recommend not doing any of these until you are an experienced middler and have a good feel for the risks involved.

If you do back "pseudo arbs" of any description, I recommend setting up a separate "bank" for these. Remember the golden rule: **Focus on the potential losses and aim to limit them.**

With a "pseudo arb" the maximum potential loss is usually the total stake on all outcomes. Therefore, you should set a fixed percentage of your "bank" – say 5% - and this will be your total stake on all the outcomes you are betting. Whether you bet "pseudo arb" at all depends on your attitude to risk, I back those with 3% expected value or more.

Finding Middles

If you want to look for Middles manually then except on very new lines, Oddschecker and Tip-pex are good starting points. Noting down the best lines available may not give you a decent middle straight away. But you will see where the market is and if it's match day and you tune in a few times, you'll be able to see which way the lines are moving and which books are leading the moves.

After that, it's a case of line shopping around books you are with which aren't on these services. I like to note down the moneyline (to win) odds as well as the handicaps since you can sometimes find good arbs from these.

However, I rarely check manually now as automated services are far more efficient. The Middles service available on ArbAlarm sends out several hundred Middles every month which makes the process a whole lot easier.

Middles are not for everybody and the risks involved may put some bettors off altogether, even though they may be experienced arbitrage traders. However, the rewards are currently significantly higher than for arbitrage. Opportunities last for longer before lines move, and average returns on capital are better too.

An Additional Middling Technique

In horse-racing, some bookmakers will pay on disqualified winners. It is worth checking with these bookmakers daily to see if you can back a few horses there in order to Lay them at Betfair or other exchange. With the correct prices you can ensure that the trade will either break-even or result in a very small profit or loss. Every now and then, horses that you have backed will win but will be disqualified. In these cases, the bookmaker will pay you out as a winner whilst the exchange will mark your Lay bet as a winner - so you get paid on both sides without taking any risk.

An alternative on this is to look for bookmakers with enhanced "place" terms - that this those bookmakers who pay out on each-way bets if your horse comes in 4th or even 5th whilst the betting exchanges only consider the 1st, 2nd and 3rd placed horses. In this case you would bet on the horse each-way at the bookmaker and then lay the same horse each-way in the Place market on Betfair or other exchange. If the horse comes in 4th or 5th, you get paid by the bookmaker and you also win your Lay bet at the exchange.

I usually don't bet more than £50 at a time on these horse trades but I've made in excess of £9000 over the last 16 month just from this method alone.

Trading In-running

Whilst there are some good opportunities for betting in-running in sports such as cricket and darts, I would warn against the temptation to try betting in-running with horse-races on exchanges. Of course, if you have a position which you need to hedge then this can be done in-running. My warning is against trying to use betting in-running as a solo technique to make money on horses.

Why?

Even if you now have the latest super gazillion Hz computer; even if you have your own 8Mb pipe to the internet, there will always be someone with better technical advantage than you.

It is rumoured that there are now teams of punters visiting racecourse with the specific intention of stealing a lead on home-based punters.

They are said to be operating from the back of a van with an laptop connected to the internet (presumably with a 3G card, or via a local pub / hotel wi-fi connection). On course there is a skilled race reader who relays the race back to the van allowing the keyboard operator to punch in backs or lays seconds ahead of the masses watching the racing on their TV's and trading via their home PC's.

A few years ago it could have been advantageous to bet in running. The majority of the country were still on 56K dial up; the majority didn't realise their PC's were being slowed down by trojans and spyware; the majority didn't even realise about time delays on William Hill Radio, Attheraces online live webcast, or even with Terrestrial TV!

(Note that there are propagation delays when transmitting live pictures via satellite. By the time an image reaches our screen it has been beamed up into space and back at least three times and has travelled nearly 150,000 miles)

Let me quote bookmaker Barry Dennis who said this of in-running betting last year:

> **Barry Dennis, however, believes it is an easy way to make money and feels the time delay is catching out many players. Dennis said:**
>
> *"If someone at the course sees a horse fall they can get on and lay it before people watching at home realise it's fallen. Similarly, four to five seconds can mean 100 yards, so while people backing in-running on a race at home might think three or four are still in contention, those at the course already know the winner.*
>
> *I have also known betting on stewards' inquiries to go on 30 seconds after the results have been announced at the course. It's a dog-eat-dog world, and when I told John McCririck about this, he asked about my ethics. I said I didn't know the meaning of the word."*

That was last year. Technology has advanced even further since then.

Using ArbAlarm Sports Arbitrage Software

There are a number of compelling reasons to use software to help you locate arbitrage trades.

- ✓ **Increased profits**
  There is no doubt that if you use ArbAlarm sports-arbitrage software properly you will make much higher profits than without.

- ✓ **Saved time**
  Using ArbAlarm sports-arbitrage software will help to save a lot of time. If you can rely upon the software to do the searching on your behalf, it frees you up to look in other places or do other things.

- ✓ **Provide tip-offs for other trades**
  This is a much overlooked benefit but it is something which has been mentioned by every trader who has contributed to writing of this book. When ArbAlarm sports-arbitrage software sends you an arbitrage trade, it very often provides tip-offs about other possible trades. For example, a soccer arbitrage trade may contain a price which you can use in one of the exchange strategies instead of the arbitrage trade of which you have been notified. The key issue is that the software is going to bring this to your attention faster than any other method of research. ArbAlarm sports-arbitrage software also allows you to choose to receive break-even trades i.e. those where the prices add up to 100% and this can be used to great effect when using the bonus-hunting techniques described earlier in this book.

- ✓ **Act as an early-warning for price-releases**
  ArbAlarm sports-arbitrage software allows you to be the first to know when a bookmaker has posted new prices on-site. This early-warning system can be of great advantage in trading strategies that require you to analyse new prices as soon as possible.
- ✓ **Provide useful stats**
  ArbAlarm's website provides some fairly useful statistics. It

actually shows you how many arbs each bookie has had in each sport each month. This is extremely powerful for research as it lets you see exactly which accounts are the most important each month. Many professional traders use this to decide where their funds should be placed ready for trading each month, and you should certainly make this a site you check regularly.

Below are the 3 websites you should check for free demos and the latest downloads of their respective software.

✓ **www.arbalarm.com - this software brings live arbitrage trades to your desktop**

✓ **www.arbsurfer.com – this software is a specialised browser developed specifically to speed up a sports-arbitrage trader's processes**

✓ **www.arbaccounts.com – this software handles all of your trading accounting needs seamlessly** www.sportsarbitrageworld.com

Reference Pages

Table of Odds vs. Percentages

You can use the following table to convert the bookmakers' prices into percentages. Then you simply add up the percentages for all possible outcomes for the event.

The UK column contains the numbers you will see when checking most UK bookmakers' price lists

The US column contains the numbers you will see when checking most US bookmakers' price lists

The EU column contains the numbers you will see when checking most European bookmakers' price lists. Some UK bookmakers also express their prices in this format.

2/7	-350	1.29	77.80
3/10	-330	1.30	76.70
1/3	-300	1.33	75.00
4/11	-275	1.36	73.33
2/5	-250	1.40	71.43
4/9	-225	1.44	69.23
1/2	-200	1.50	66.67
8/15	-190	1.53	65.50
4/7	-175	1.57	63.64
8/13	-161	1.65	61.90
2/3	-150	1.67	60.00
8/11	-137	1.73	57.89
4/5	-125	1.80	55.56
5/6	-120	1.83	54.55
9/10	-111	1.90	52.63
10/11	-110	1.91	52.38
1/1	100	2.00	50.00
21/20	105	2.05	48.78
11/10	110	2.10	47.62
10/9	111	2.11	47.37
6/5	120	2.20	45.45
5/4	125	2.25	44.44
13/10	130	2.30	43.48
27/20	135	2.35	42.55
11/8	137	2.37	42.11
7/5	140	2.40	41.67
3/2	150	2.50	40.00
8/5	160	2.60	38.46
13/8	162	2.62	38.10
17/10	170	2.70	37.04
7/4	175	2.75	36.36
9/5	180	2.80	35.71
15/8	187	2.87	34.78
19/10	190	2.90	34.48
2/1	200	3.00	33.33
21/10	210	3.10	32.26
11/5	220	3.20	31.25
9/4	225	3.25	30.77

23/10	230	3.30	30.30
12/5	240	3.40	29.41
5/2	250	3.50	28.57
13/5	260	3.60	27.78
27/10	270	3.70	27.03
11/4	275	3.75	26.67
14/5	280	3.80	26.32
3/1	300	4.00	25.00
10/3	333	4.33	23.08
7/2	350	4.50	22.22
4/1	400	5.00	20.00
9/2	450	5.50	18.18
5/1	500	6.00	16.67
11/2	550	6.50	15.38
6/1	600	7.00	14.29
13/2	650	7.50	13.33
7/1	700	8.00	12.50
15/2	750	8.50	11.76
8/1	800	9.00	11.11
17/2	850	9.50	10.53
9/1	900	10.00	10.00
10/1	1000	11.00	9.09
11/1	1100	12.00	8.33
12/1	1200	13.00	7.69
14/1	1400	15.00	6.67
16/1	1600	17.00	5.88
18/1	1800	19.00	5.26
20/1	2000	21.00	4.76
22/1	2200	23.00	4.35
25/1	2500	26.00	3.85
28/1	2800	29.00	3.45
33/1	3300	34.00	2.94
40/1	4000	41.00	2.44
50/1	5000	51.00	1.96
66/1	6600	67.00	1.49
80/1	8000	81.00	1.23
100/1	10000	101.00	0.99

Terminology

10 Cent Line
The money line difference (10 cents) between what a bettor would lay with the favourite or take back with the underdog; see Dime Line

20 Cent Line
The money line difference (20 cents) between what a bettor would lay with the favourite or take back with the underdog

2-ball / 3-ball 18-hole match-ups
A golfing bet that involves predicting which player from either a group of two or three will shoot the lowest score over 18 holes.

72-hole match bets
A golf wager, where the bookmaker will match up two players of similar ability, with the winner being the player who shoots the lowest score over the tournaments 4 rounds.

Across the Card
Meaning to bet in doubles etc. on simultaneous races.

Accumulator
A bet involving more than one event with the winnings from each selection going onto the next in chronological order. All selections must win for a return, unless the accumulator is part of a specially-branded wager which has consolation dividends. Also known as "Roll Up" or "All On".

All Up To Win
In horse races of four runners or less, the place portion of an each-way wager goes on to win as there is no place betting returned in such cases

Ante-Post
Also known as "Future". Betting on an event at least a day in advance. This can be a year or more before the event. If your selection does not take part in the race, match or event, you lose your money. This risk is often compensated by higher odds.

Any to Come (ATC)
A form of betting contingent upon money in hand from the original
investment. "Stakes On" is a variation meaning re-invest original stake.

Asian Handicap
A style of betting which removes the chances of a draw and is the same
as the way Americans bet on the spread. Sides are awarded anywhere
between a fraction of a goal start to 3 goals dependent on how good or
bad they are. The bookies may also use a half point start which
effectively eliminates the draw (used in the Far East).

Backed
When a bookmaker takes a lot of money on one particular side, it is said
that this team has been heavily backed. It is where the punter has put his
money on.

Banker
A selection that is considered the most certain among a number of
selections.

Bar
Odds for an event are often quoted for a number of participants and then
there is the statement, 20/1 bar or 33/1 bar. This means that there are
other participants or likely participants in the event who are outsiders
priced at 20/1 or longer in the first example or at least 33/1 in the second
example.

Betting Exchanges
Betting exchanges cut out the bookmaker and enable bettors who want to
lay bets (like a bookmaker) and those who want to back horses to come
together. Betting exchanges make their money by charging a
commission.

Betting Percentages
Betting percentages show whether the odds are in favour of bettors or
bookmakers. A neutral outcome would be for the percentage to be 100%
but bookmakers have to make a profit and therefore there is usually
always an element of over round, i.e. a margin favour of bookmakers.
Typically the percentage of odds from any bookmaker will be between

115% and 125%, though this can be lower or higher, largely depending on the number of participants. But, by considering the best odds from all bookmakers, the percentage in favour of bookmakers is often sharply reduced and can even swing directly into bettors' favour by going below 100%.

Bettor
Describes someone who bets, originated in America. The British term is punter.

Bismarck
From the battleship Bismarck who was sunk, an expression used by Channel 4 Racing and bookmaker Barry Dennis to denote the likeliest short-priced horse of the day who will get sunk (i.e. not win).

Board Prices
The boards this refers to are the on-course bookmakers' boards on which odds are displayed. The odds vary depending on demand and the changing odds are relayed to off-course betting outlets.

Bookmaker
Betting organisation or person who takes bets.

Canadian
A full-cover multiple bet, with five selections from five different events. A Canadian has 26 bets - 10 doubles, 10 trebles, five four-folds and one accumulator. A minimum of two selections have to win for you to receive a return.

Circled Game
Game where action is limited due to uncertainties about weather, injuries, etc.

Conditional Bet
A bet which is dependent on a specific condition being fulfilled. e.g. 'if win', 'if lose', 'any to come' etc

Combination
An algebraic term denoting that a series of groups is to be taken from a

larger group without regard to order. It is also loosely used as an instruction to permute a series of forecasts.

Concessions
Special terms offered by bookmakers more generous than normal to attract more bettors - the bookmakers' equivalent of hold a sale.

Correct score
A wager that involves correctly predicting the final score of a game.

Cover to Win
A wager in which the selection is backed to win a fixed amount, the liability being dependent on the starting price.

Credit Bet
A bet accepted by a bookmaker where no cash has been deposited.

Credit Limit
The amount that a backer is allowed to lose in any one week's business by the bookmaker before settlement is required.

Cumulative Odds
An Ante-Post term denoting full accumulative odds for a double event as at starting price.

Daily Tote Double
A double event in the Totalisator pool operated on the third and fifth races at any meeting. Backer has to forecast, by name, the winner of each of the two races. Unnamed selections, such as favourites, are not accepted.

Daily Tote Treble
A Totalisator pool operated usually on the second, fourth and sixth races at a meeting. Backer has to forecast, by name, the winner of each of the three races. Unnamed selections, such as favourites, are not accepted.

Debit Bet
No cash is exchanged in this debit bet but the bookmaker has the right to debit the punter's bank account.

Dime Line

Slang used to designate the 10 cent money line. The money line difference (10 cents) between what a bettor would lay with the favourite or take back with the underdog; see 10 Cent Line.

Dog

Underdog

Dividend

The return for a single winning unit usually on the tote but bookmakers also offer dividend prices.

Double

A two-leg accumulator with the winnings from the first selection automatically going onto the second selection in chronological order. Both selections need to win for a return.

Each-way

Betting for a win and a place. A varying percentage of the win odds is paid for a place which can be the first two home, the first three or the first four, depending on the number of runners. In five to seven runner races, the usual bookmaker terms are a quarter of the win odds and two places, from eight to 12 runner races the terms are one fifth of the odds and three places, for 12 to 15 runners in handicaps it is one quarter the odds and three places, for 16 and more runners in handicaps it is a quarter the odds and four places. Bookmakers can offer more generous terms on big races.

Favourite

The participant mostly likely to win according to the odds, having the shortest odds in an event. You can have joint favourites when two runners share the shortest odds and co favourites when more than two runners jointly have the shortest odds.

First Goalscorer

A bet placed on a player to score the first goal in a game.

First Tryscorer - A bet placed on a player to score the first try in a rugby match.

Forecast

This bet consists of two or more selections from one event, and is available on horseracing and greyhound racing, subject to a minimum number of runners taking part. To win your two selections must finish in first and second place, in the order you specify. Forecasts are available in singles, doubles and trebles. Reverse forecasts are also available whereby your two selections can finish in either order. The stake for this bet is doubled.

Grand Slam

The four major tennis tournaments: Wimbledon, Australian Open, French Open, and U.S. Open. Also the four major golf tournaments: The Masters, U.S. Open, British Open and the PGA Championship (Professional Golf Association). Also in baseball, a homerun with the bases loaded, scoring four runs.

Grand Salami

A slang word for the over/under total for the combined score of all the hockey contests on the schedule for that day

Halftime Line

A line on only the first half, or only the second half scoring of a US football or basketball game

Half time result

A wager that involves correctly predicting the result of a game at half time.

Handicap betting

A handicap is a race in which the participants have to carry differing weights which will make all their chances theoretically equal. A betting handicap attempts to do the same by giving a team or individual a head start for betting purposes.

Hedging

Reducing exposure by placing opposing bets. Arbitrage is the most refined form of hedging as it not only eliminates risk, but also allows for a built-in profit.

Heinz
A full-cover multiple bet, with six selections from six different events. A Heinz has 57 bets - 15 doubles, 20 trebles, 15 four-folds, six five-folds and one accumulator. A minimum of two selections have to win for you to receive a return.

Home Field Advantage
Edge the home team is expected to have as a result of familiarity with the playing area, favourable demographics and effect of travel on the visiting team

Hook
Half point in pointspreads

Hoops
A slang term for Basketball

In-running betting
Some bookmakers offer odds during an event with the odds fluctuating according to the state of play.

Jolly
Another expression for the favourite.

Joint Favourites
When a bookmaker cannot split two teams for favouritism - for example, Arsenal and Manchester United may both be joint favourites at 6/4 to win the English Premiership.

Juice
Bookmaker's commission, most often refers to the 11 to 10 football bettors lay on straight wagers. Also known as vigorish

Knock out
This is where an on-course bookmaker or bookmakers keeps lengthening the odds on offer about a horse, either believing it will not win or for others to be able back that horse at a bigger odds than it should be off course.

Layer
Another expression for a bookmaker, someone who lays, i.e. accepts, bets.

Laying Off
Bookmaker passing on all or part of a bet to another bookie

Lengthen
When a bookmaker sees that no-one is backing a particular side, he may choose to lengthen the odds available.

Levels
The price of evens (1/1, 2.00 or +100)

Lines
Handicaps, pointspreads and odds offered to the punter.

Listed Pitcher (LP)
The pitcher or pitchers listed by Las Vegas oddsmakers as probable starting pitchers for a scheduled baseball game

Maximum payouts
These vary from bookmaker to bookmaker and are worth checking if you like doing accumulative bets.

Middle
To win both sides of a game. For example, if you bet the underdog +3 1/2 and the favourite -2 1/2 and the favourite wins by 3, you've middled the book. The book has been middled.

MLB
Major League Baseball

Moneyline
The amount you must bet to win 100 or the amount you win if you bet 100

MVP
Most Valuable Player. Leagues give MVP Awards to the best regular-season and to the outstanding player in championship games or series

Money Lists
In Golf, the list of the amount of official money won by each golfer on their respective tours.

Monkey
Slang expression for £500.

Nap
The best bet of the day according to a pundit or tipster.

NBA
National Basketball Association

NCAA
National Collegiate Athletic Association

Neutral Site
Arena, court or field where neither side has a home field advantage

NFL
National Football League

NHL
National Hockey League

Number Spread
An index spread based on the number of runs, goals and points scored in an event.

Odds
Traditional odds from British bookmakers are expressed in fractional form. Using traditional odds, the return on a £10 bet at odds of 5/1 is £50, plus you receive your stake back, making a total of £60.
Decimal is a different way of expressing odds. Decimal odds make it easier to calculate your returns. You simply multiply the decimal odds

offered by the amount you are staking. For multiple bets, multiply the decimal odds together and then multiply that by your stake. Using decimal odds, 5/1 would be expressed as 6, indicating the total return, including your stake, from a bet - therefore the £10 bet would return the same total of £60.

Odds-Against
If you are betting at odds-against your stake is smaller than the amount that you are going to win, i.e. if you wager £5 at odds of 5/4, you will win £6.25, with the total return, including your stake, being £11.25.

Odds Compiler
The person working for the bookmaker who sets the odds following research and his own feelings.

Odds-on
If you are betting at odds-on your stake is bigger than the amount that you are going to win, i.e. if you wager £5 at odds of 4/5, you will win £4, with the total return, including your stake, being £9.

Outsider
The opposite to the favourite, usually to be found at lengthy odds.

Over Round
See Percentages. Over round is the percentage in bookmakers' favour.

Over/Under
A bet on whether the combined total of the points/goals scored by the two teams will exceed or be less than a specified number

Overlay
When the odds on a proposition are in favour of the bettor rather than the house

Overtime
The continuance of a contest that is tied at the end of regulation time until a winner is determined or the maximum number of overtime periods have expired

Patent

A Patent is a full-cover multiple bet with singles. It consists of three selections and is made up of three singles, three doubles and one treble. With this bet only one selection has to win for you to receive a return.

Parlay

The US term for accumulators i.e. bet with two or more teams where all the teams must win for the bettor to be successful

Percentages

Bookmakers set their odds according to percentages, the lower the percentage, the better deal the punter is getting.

To calculate the percentage each price is worth, add a point and divide into 100. So 3/1 becomes four into 100, equals 25.

A perfectly round book, with each price representing the true chance, would total 100.

A book totalling 125 would be 25 percent over-round and give bookmakers a theoretical profit of 20 percent (25 divided by 125). In general, the bigger the field, the more the percentage favours the bookmakers.

For an arbitrage to exist, the book should total less than 100% and this situation is also known as an Under Round

Pointspread

An American term for handicap i.e. the start that the favourite gives to the outsider

Pucks

A slang word used to indicate the game of hockey

Punter

British expression for someone who bets.

Rails bookmaker

British racecourses have different areas of the course where bookmakers are placed. Rails bookmakers are traditionally the most influential, being placed on the between the Club enclosure and the Tattersalls enclosure. Two years ago they were allowed to display their odds on boards, having previously had to rely on communicating their odds by shouting them out.

Rule 4

If a horse is withdrawn shortly before the start of a British horserace and there is insufficient time to form a new betting market, then bookmakers are entitled to deduct money from winnings bets. The deductions are listed below:

3/10 or longer odds 75p in the £
2/5 to 1/3 70p
8/15 to 4/9 65p
8/13 to 4/7 60p
4/5 to 4/6 55p
20/21 to 5/6 50p
odds to 6/5 45p
5/4 to 6/4 40p
13/8 to 7/4 35p
15/8 to 9/4 30p
5/2 to 3/1 25p
10/3 to 4/1 20p
9/2 to 11/2 15p
6/1 to 9/1 10p
10/1 to 14/1 5p
14/1 unchanged

Ryder Cup

A golf tournament between American and European golfers that is staged every two years

Scalper

American term for arbitrageur i.e. one who attempts to profit from the differences in odds from book to book by betting both sides of the same game at different prices

Side

To win one side and tie the other. For example, if you lay -2 1/2 and take 3 on the same game and the favourite wins by 3 you have sided the book. The book has been sided.

Set Betting
A wager that involves correctly predicting the final set score of a game.

Single
A single is one bet on one selection, player or team in a particular event. Your selection must win that event for you to get a return.

Soft Line
A wagering line that is not current with the true posted line. A line that has been adjusted or moved as a result of action and does not reflect the true line as posted.

Spread Betting
Not to be confused with spreads. A volatile type of betting that could see the punter reap huge returns or equally large losses.

Stake
Amount of money you bet with a bookmaker and which you will lose if the result is not as you predicted.

Stanley Cup
NHL Championship

Starting Price
The official odds for a horse in a race calculated at the time of the off by starting-price reporters at British and Irish racecourses.

Steamer
A runner whose odds are rapidly shortened by bookmakers because of continual support.

Sudden Death
An overtime period in which the first contestant to score is declared the winner of the contest

Supremacy
Spreads based upon the margin of victory between teams of individuals.

Superbowl
NFL Championship game

Teaser
A bet on 2 or more teams where the line on each team is adjusted in the favour of the bettor. Like a Parlay, all selections must be correct for the teaser to win

Tic-tac
The hand signals which bookmakers on racecourses used to communicate with.

Tipsters
People who are paid by newspapers or bettors to give betting advice.

Tissue
The tissue is the odds advice given to bookmakers by professional odds compilers. With the advent of betting exchanges, this has become less important.

Top batsman
The highest scoring batsman for one particular team.

Total over/under
A wager that involves predicting whether the score of a game will go over or under a predetermined level.

Totalisator
The Totalisator is run by the Horse Race Totalisator Board and is operated on all racecourses. It operates as a pool wherein investors' money, less a fixed percentage, is shared between backers of successful selections.

Tout
A person who frequents training grounds for the purpose of gaining information about the capabilities of the horses and which he passes on for a fee.

Treble

A three-leg accumulator. Any winnings from the first selection automatically go on to the second and then if that wins onto the third in chronological order. For you to be successful all three selections have to win.

Tricast

A Tricast consists of three or more selections from one event, and is available on horseracing and greyhound racing, subject to a minimum number of runners participating. In this bet you must successfully nominate the first three past the post in the correct order. Tricasts can be placed "straight" with three selections, or "combinations" (permed) with three or more selections. Tricasts are available as singles only.

Trixie

A Trixie is a multiple bet made up of three selections in different events. A Trixie is made up of four bets - three doubles and one treble. To get a return, a minimum of two selections have to win.

Underdog

America term for the outsider i.e. the team that receives the point start in a handicap.

Value

Signifies to a punter that the bookmaker is offering a price which is better than the true probability of the outcome

Vigorish

Bookmaker's commission, most often refers to the 11 to 10 football bettors lay on straight wagers. Also known as juice.

Volatility

Term used to express the range of possible results in a particular Index bet.

Void Bet

A bet which is declared invalid. The stake is returned without deduction

Wager
A transaction on any event where an amount of money is staked.

WBA
World Boxing Association

WBC
World Boxing Council

Winning margin
A wager that involves predicting the winning margin of one team over another.

Wise Guy
Established and successful sports bettor

WNBA
Women's National Basketball Association

World Series
MLB championship; The final seven games of the baseball playoffs between the two league champions to determine the world champion.

Yankee
A multiple bet that consists of four selections with six doubles, four trebles and one four-timer - 11 bets in total.